The Politics and Economics of Brexit

T0270759

The British referendum on continuing membership of the European Union (EU) in June 2016 represented a turning point in the relationship between the United Kingdom (UK) and the EU. This book investigates the implications of Brexit for the EU and the UK, placing this assessment in the context of the long-term evolution of UK–EU relations. The authors relate these findings to debates within the literature on EU policy-making, comparative politics, and political economy.

The first part of this comprehensive volume explores the implications of Brexit for key policy areas, namely the single market, finance, and migration. The policies selected are those in which the consequences of Brexit are likely to be most significant because they are linked to the 'four freedoms' in the Single Market. The second part of the book explores important 'horizontal' or thematic issues, namely lessons from Brexit for theories of integration, the balance of power in the EU amongst the main member states post-Brexit, the evolution of the domestic political contestation in the EU, and the impact of Brexit on domestic politics in the UK.

This book was originally published as a special issue of the *Journal of European Public Policy*.

Simon Bulmer is Professor of European Politics at the University of Sheffield, UK. His recent publications include *Germany and the European Union: the reluctant hegemon?* (2018, with William Paterson) and *Politics in the European Union*, 4th edition (2015, with Ian Bache, Stephen George, and Owen Parker).

Lucia Quaglia is Professor of Political Science at the University of Bologna, Italy. Her most recent books include *The Political Economy of Banking Union* (2016, with D. Howarth) and *The European Union and Global Financial Regulation* (2014).

Journal of European Public Policy Series

Series Editors

Jeremy Richardson is Emeritus Fellow at Nuffield College, Oxford University, UK and Adjunct Professor in the National Centre for Research on Europe at the University of Canterbury, Christchurch, New Zealand.

Berthold Rittberger is Professor and Chair of International Relations at the Geschwister-Scholl-Institute of Political Science at the University of Munich, Germany.

This series seeks to bring together some of the finest edited works on European Public Policy. Reprinting from special issues of the *Journal of European Public Policy*, the focus is on using a wide range of social sciences approaches, both qualitative and quantitative, to gain a comprehensive and definitive understanding of Public Policy in Europe.

Transforming Food and Agricultural Policy
Post-exceptionalism in Public Policy
Edited by Carsten Daugbjerg and Peter Feindt

EU Socio-Economic Governance since the Crisis
The European Semester in Theory and Practice
Edited by Jonathan Zeitlin and Amy Verdun

The Future of the Social Investment State
Policies, Outcomes and Politics
Edited by Marius R. Busemeyer, Caroline de la Porte, Julian L. Garritzmann and Emmanuele Pavolini

The Politics and Economics of Brexit
Edited by Simon Bulmer and Lucia Quaglia

For more information about this series, please visit: https://www.routledge.com/Journal-of-European-Public-Policy-Special-Issues-as-Books/book-series/JEPPSPIBS

The Politics and Economics of Brexit

Edited by
Simon Bulmer and Lucia Quaglia

Routledge
Taylor & Francis Group

LONDON AND NEW YORK

First published 2019
by Routledge
2 Park Square, Milton Park, Abingdon, Oxon, OX14 4RN, UK

and by Routledge
52 Vanderbilt Avenue, New York, NY 10017, USA

First issued in paperback 2020

Routledge is an imprint of the Taylor & Francis Group, an informa business

Chapters 1–6, 8 © 2019 Taylor & Francis
Chapter 7 © 2018 Paul Taggart and Aleks Szczerbiak. Originally
published as Open Access.

British Library Cataloguing-in-Publication Data
A catalogue record for this book is available from the British Library

ISBN 13: 978-0-367-58439-9 (pbk)
ISBN 13: 978-1-138-38985-4 (hbk)

Typeset in Myriad Pro
by codeMantra

Publisher's Note
The publisher accepts responsibility for any inconsistencies that may
have arisen during the conversion of this book from journal articles to
book chapters, namely the possible inclusion of journal terminology.

Disclaimer
Every effort has been made to contact copyright holders for their
permission to reprint material in this book. The publishers would
be grateful to hear from any copyright holder who is not here
acknowledged and will undertake to rectify any errors or omissions in
future editions of this book.

Contents

Citation Information

The chapters in this book were originally published in the *Journal of European Public Policy*, volume 25, issue 8 (August 2018). When citing this material, please use the original page numbering for each article, as follows:

Chapter 1
Introduction: The politics and economics of Brexit
Simon Bulmer and Lucia Quaglia
Journal of European Public Policy, volume 25, issue 8 (August 2018)
pp. 1089–1098

Chapter 2
Regulatory alignment and divergence after Brexit
Kenneth A. Armstrong
Journal of European Public Policy, volume 25, issue 8 (August 2018)
pp. 1099–1117

Chapter 3
Brexit and the battle for financial services
David Howarth and Lucia Quaglia
Journal of European Public Policy, volume 25, issue 8 (August 2018)
pp. 1118–1136

Chapter 4
Brexit and the perils of 'Europeanised' migration
James Dennison and Andrew Geddes
Journal of European Public Policy, volume 25, issue 8 (August 2018)
pp. 1137–1153

Chapter 5
Brexit: differentiated disintegration in the European Union
Frank Schimmelfennig
Journal of European Public Policy, volume 25, issue 8 (August 2018)
pp. 1154–1173

Chapter 6

Back to the future? Franco-German bilateralism in Europe's post-Brexit union
Ulrich Krotz and Joachim Schild
Journal of European Public Policy, volume 25, issue 8 (August 2018)
pp. 1174–1193

Chapter 7

Putting Brexit into perspective: the effect of the Eurozone and migration crises and Brexit on Euroscepticism in European states
Paul Taggart and Aleks Szczerbiak
Journal of European Public Policy, volume 25, issue 8 (August 2018)
pp. 1194–1214

Chapter 8

Taking back control: the political implications of Brexit
Andrew Gamble
Journal of European Public Policy, volume 25, issue 8 (August 2018)
pp. 1215–1232

For any permission-related enquiries please visit:
http://www.tandfonline.com/page/help/permissions

Notes on Contributors

Kenneth A. Armstrong is Professor of European Law at the University of Cambridge, UK. He is also a Fellow of Sidney Sussex College, University of Cambridge, UK. His book *Governing Social Inclusion: Europeanization through Policy Coordination* (2010) won the 2011 UACES Best Book Prize.

Simon Bulmer is Professor of European Politics at the University of Sheffield, UK. His recent publications include *Germany and the European Union: the reluctant hegemon?* (2018, with William Paterson) and *Politics in the European Union*, 4th edition (2015, with Ian Bache, Stephen George, and Owen Parker).

James Dennison is Research Fellow in the Migration Policy Centre at the European University Institute (EUI), Florence, Italy. There, he leads the Observatory of Public Attitudes to Migration. His research interests include attitudinal formation and electoral behaviour.

Andrew Gamble is Professor of Politics at the University of Sheffield, UK. His research interests lie in British politics, political economy, and political thought. He seeks to understand politics by exploring the complex interrelationships between state and economy, and the ideas, policies, and institutions through which these are expressed.

Andrew Geddes is Director of the Migration Policy Centre and holds the Chair in Migration Studies at EUI, Florence, Italy. Prior to joining EUI he was Professor of Politics at the University of Sheffield, UK. His current research focuses on inter- and intra-regional comparison of migration governance with a focus on Asia-Pacific, Europe, North America, and South America.

David Howarth is Professor of Political Economy at the University of Luxembourg, Luxembourg City, Luxembourg and a former Jean Monnet Chair at the University of Edinburgh, UK. His research topics are the national banking system, financial regulation, financial lobbies, economic and monetary union, and the Euro crisis.

Ulrich Krotz is Professor of International Relations. He holds the Chair in International Relations in the Department of Social and Political Sciences, and in the Robert Schuman Centre for Advanced Studies, at EUI, Florence, Italy. He is also Director of the EUI's programme on Europe in the World.

Lucia Quaglia is Professor of Political Science at the University of Bologna, Italy. Her most recent books include *The Political Economy of Banking Union* (2016, with D. Howarth) and *The European Union and Global Financial Regulation* (2014).

Joachim Schild is Professor of Political Science/Comparative Politics at the University of Trier, Germany. His research interests are French European policy, Franco-German relations, the Europeanisation of nation states, the political economy of European integration, and the political system of the French Fifth Republic.

Frank Schimmelfennig is Professor of European Politics, and a member of the Center for Comparative and International Studies, at ETH Zurich, Switzerland. His main research interest lies in the theory of European integration and, more specifically, in EU enlargement, differentiated integration, democracy promotion, and democratisation.

Aleks Szczerbiak is Professor of Politics & Contemporary European Studies, and Director of Doctoral Studies for Law, Politics and Sociology, at the University of Sussex, UK. His research expertise is in East European politics, Euroscepticism, party politics, Poland, and transitional justice. He is the co-convenor (with Paul Taggart) of the European Referendums, Elections and Parties Network (EPERN).

Paul Taggart is Professor of Politics, Jean Monnet Chair, and Director of the Sussex European Institute at the University of Sussex, UK. His research expertise is in domestic politics of European integration, Euroscepticism, political parties, and populism. He is the co-convenor (with Aleks Szczerbiak) of EPERN.

The politics and economics of Brexit

Simon Bulmer and Lucia Quaglia

Introduction

The British referendum on continuing membership of the European Union (EU) in June 2016 represented a turning point in the relationship between the United Kingdom (UK) and the EU. The result – a 51.9% to 48.1% victory for Leave voters on a high turnout of 72.2% – was accepted by Prime Minister David Cameron as a defeat; he resigned. In March 2017, the British government under Prime Minister Theresa May invoked Article 50 of the Treaty on European Union, officially beginning the negotiations of UK withdrawal from the EU – the Brexit process. The economic and political effects of Brexit will be far-reaching for the UK and the EU and warrant scholarly examination. This collection has two main aims: to investigate the implications of Brexit for the EU and the UK, placing this assessment in the context of the long-term evolution of UK-EU relations; and to draw some lessons from it, relating these findings to debates within the literature on EU policy-making, comparative politics and political economy.

Brexit raises a set of important questions addressed by this collection: (i) what are the repercussions of Brexit for the EU, to be precise its policies, the relations between member states and the domestic contestation of the EU? (ii) what are the consequence of Brexit for the UK, specifically for British politics and the British economy? (iii) What are the implication of Brexit for theories of EU integration? The papers address these questions. The material is organized into two parts. The first explores the implications of Brexit for key policy areas, namely the single market, finance and migration. The policies selected are those in which the consequences of Brexit are likely to be most significant because they are linked to the 'four freedoms' in the Single Market. The second part explores important 'horizontal' or thematic issues, namely lessons from Brexit for theories of integration, the balance of power in the EU amongst the main member states post-Brexit, the evolution of the domestic political contestation in the EU, and the impact of Brexit on domestic politics in the UK.

In this short introductory essay, we first provide an understanding of the background to Brexit. We then discuss the dynamics of the Brexit negotiations, and finally present the main findings of the papers, teasing out some common themes. Two main caveats are in order. First, for reasons of space, there are important policy areas that are not included in this collection, such as trade and foreign policy. The negotiations on the future relations between the UK and the EU in these policy areas have barely started; hence assessment would be premature. Second, some assessments put forward in the contributions can only be provisional and will partly depend on the final deal agreed by the UK and the EU. However, the trends and challenges highlighted by the various contributions will influence the course of the Brexit negotiations, their final outcome and UK-EU relations after Brexit.

Understanding the background to Brexit

The UK's relationship with European integration has been turbulent. The UK government refused to engage with the 1950 Schuman Declaration for integration of the coal and steel industries. In November 1955 it withdrew from the Spaak Committee preparing the eventual European Economic Community. Britain considered itself a world power and Europe only one of its spheres of influence. Prime Minister Harold Macmillan's effort to undertake a post-Suez policy shift by applying for membership of the European Communities (EC) failed in cabinet due to ministerial divisions (Tratt 1996: 123–7). When it was presented to cabinet again in April 1961 – after a re-shuffle – it succeeded (Tratt 1996: 168–80). However, the French President, Charles de Gaulle, rejected the application in January 1963. While accession negotiations had been under way in Brussels the Labour leader, Hugh Gaitskell, declared his opposition at the October 1962 party conference. Membership would mean 'the end of Britain as an independent state' and 'the end of a thousand years of British history' (Young 1998: 163). Hugo Young (1998: 161) dubbed Gaitskell the first 'Euro-sceptic'. These events set the tone for what followed.

Some of the challenges in the UK-EU relationship have come from the EU itself: the two rejections of membership by de Gaulle (in 1963 and 1965); the policy 'misfits' that the European budgetary system and the Common Agricultural Policy presented for the UK; and the other member states developing policies at odds with UK government preferences, resulting in the need for various policy opt-outs. Other clashes have come from a kind of mutual misunderstanding or conflicting values: successive UK governments' failure to come to terms with integration as a political project; the repeated attraction of Atlanticist options rather than EU ones; and an adversarial approach to EU diplomacy rather than alliance-building with EU partners. However, it has been the controversy within British politics that has been especially persistent.

Divisions between and within parties, exacerbated by adversarial politics within Westminster, have been an enduring feature. Appeals to maintaining national (i.e., external) sovereignty and (internal) parliamentary sovereignty have been recurrent themes in British political rhetoric on European integration. It has been rare that political elites have had the opportunity to demonstrate EU benefits and much more frequent that the EU has been a matter of controversy. Just as Mrs Thatcher's government had successfully advocated neoliberal policies in the EU as a protagonist of the Single Market in the mid-1980s, she developed a more hostile position to integration in light of EU spillover towards monetary union and social policy in the 1988 Bruges speech (Thatcher 1988). Prime Minister Blair's efforts at a step-change in the UK's relationship with the EU was not without achievement but the expected charm offensive on public opinion never occurred because it was to be linked with the prospect of joining the single currency: a step never taken.

The European issue's persistence has been due to several competing and evolving views of Britain and its relationship with Europe (Bulmer and James 2018). In the early years a conservative appeal to Britain's global and Commonwealth relations introduced one basis of opposition to membership. More recently, this conservative position evolved into a more populist Euroscepticism with its origins in Mrs Thatcher's Bruges speech and the divisions that opened up with the Maastricht Treaty. In particular, the UK's September 1992 exit from the Exchange Rate Mechanism – called 'the first Brexit' by Keegan et al. (2017) – reinforced this emergent cleavage within the Conservative Party. The United Kingdom Independence Party (UKIP) became the outriders of this national-conservative position.

The economic benefits of integration formed much of the original vision of a centre-right 'trading' vision of integration: one espoused by Conservative prime ministers Macmillan and Heath. This perspective was solidified by Mrs Thatcher's efforts to export ideas of liberalization to the EU via the Single Market. However, the Conservative divisions following the Bruges speech (above) have been compounded by splits within this neoliberal view of the EU. Some politicians call for a 'global Britain' because the EU is deemed an obstacle to liberal trade.

On the left of the party spectrum the debates of the 1970s and 1980s concerned whether economic and social welfare could best be delivered inside or outside the EC/EU. This conundrum split Labour when it entered government in 1974. They could only be resolved after re-negotiating the terms of membership. The subsequent 1975 referendum, at which 67% voted to stay in the EC, helped paper over intra-party divisions. Those preferring the national route took a dominant role in the Labour Party for much of the 1980s (withdrawal was party policy from 1980 to 1987/88). That current party leader, Jeremy Corbyn, was in the 'national' camp, whereas many of his MPs from the Blairite generation followed a pro-EU approach to economic and social welfare, explains the party's travails from the 1975 referendum to the present.

These evolving divisions offer some explanation to the lead-in to the referendum. The 2010–15 coalition government combined the Liberal Democrats, the most consistently pro-European party, with the post-Maastricht, more Euro-sceptic version of the Conservative Party. European policy dissent was rife. From these divisions and electoral concerns about the rise of UKIP came David Cameron's Bloomberg speech (2015), in which he set out his vision for the UK, argued for a new settlement with the EU and promised a referendum thereafter. After his re-election in May 2015, he had to operationalize the promises. Re-negotiations culminated in a European Council agreement in February 2016. To many of his backbenchers and key parts of the print media, the achievements were underwhelming. This judgement set the tone for a referendum campaign during which his own party was divided, while Jeremy Corbyn's commitment to remaining in the EU seemed un-enthusiastic.

Delivering Brexit was the challenge for incoming Prime Minister Theresa May. She has found herself confronted with a two-level game. On one level she has to find agreement with EU partners around a set of principles laid out in her speeches (below). Yet she also has to manage the continuing divisions outlined above that run right through the heart of her party. That she has to rely on the support of Northern Ireland's Democratic Unionist Party (DUP) has weakened her position further and adds complexity to the question of the Irish border. Indeed it exacerbates a further domestic dimension, namely territoriality, for voters in Scotland, Northern Ireland and London voted to remain in the EU.

The dynamics of the Brexit negotiations

In the wake of the referendum Theresa May calculated that she had to make a clear break from the EU to secure the support of her Eurosceptic backbenchers. She interpreted the referendum result as a clear signal that voters wanted the government to control EU immigration, suggesting a so-called 'hard' Brexit, which would leave the UK outside the single market and the customs union.

In her January 2017 speech at Lancaster House, the Prime Minister (May 2017a) outlined the government's negotiating objectives for Brexit. The speech ruled out membership of the single market and customs union, calling instead for a 'Global Britain' to strike a free trade deal with the EU and new trade agreements with other countries. Other important objectives for the government were to: take back control of immigration and British laws; end the jurisdiction of the European Court of Justice; avoid a 'hard border' with Ireland; and guarantee the rights of EU citizens living in Britain, and the rights of British nationals in other member states. In February 2017, the UK government (2017) issued a White Paper that further elaborated the points made in the Lancaster House Speech. In March 2017, the UK government invoked Article 50 and the negotiations on withdrawal began.

The EU negotiating guidelines adopted formally by the European Council (2017) in April 2017 outlined the 'core principles' for the negotiations and called for a 'phased approach'. The guidelines made clear that 'a non-member of the Union, that does not live up to the same obligations as a member, cannot have the same rights and enjoy the same benefits as a member' and that the four freedoms of the Single Market were indivisible, thus there could be no 'cherry picking'. The document also argued that negotiations should be divided into two phases: the first concerning the terms of exit and the second concerning the future of UK-EU relations. The second phase would start after 'sufficient progress' had been made in the first phase. Finally, the EU made clear that there would be no separate negotiations between individual member states and the UK.

In the same month, the European Parliament (which has the power of assent concerning the agreements on withdrawal and future UK-EU relations) endorsed the core principles and the phased approach outlined by the European Council. The EP (2017) reaffirmed that 'membership of the internal market and the customs union entails acceptance of the four freedoms, the jurisdiction of the Court of Justice of the European Union, general budgetary contributions and adherence to the European Union's common commercial policy'. It stressed the obligations concerning the UK's budgetary contributions and the treatment of EU nationals living in the UK. Finally, it warned against 'any bilateral arrangement' between one or several member states and the UK in the areas of EU competence.

In the first stage of Brexit negotiations, the main issues discussed were: (i) the UK's contribution to the EU budget, the winding down of spending programmes in the UK and the division of assets and pension liabilities; (ii) the acquired rights, healthcare and other social obligations for EU nationals living in UK, and UK nationals living in EU, (iii) border arrangements concerning Northern Ireland and Gibraltar.

Prime Minister May's gamble on a general election (June 2017), supposedly to strengthen her negotiating hand, backfired for the Conservative Party and resulted in the need for the DUP's parliamentary support to maintain a working majority. The Conservatives' alienation of some Remain voters was one of many factors in the election result. The government's Brexit vision became more ambiguous due to the Conservative Party's division and parliamentary difficulties. Chancellor of the Exchequer Phillip Hammond called for the need to maintain access to the Single Market, suggesting some backtracking on the 'clean break' with the EU. Other ministers insisted on existing policy.

In September 2017, approaching the most critical step of the first phase of the negotiations, May (2017b) gave a speech in Florence, pledging to honour the financial commitments that the UK made during the period of membership; offering to write legal protections for EU citizens living in the UK into the actual exit treaty; accepting a role for the ECJ in settling rights disputes; recognizing the importance of the issue of the Irish border; and calling for a transition period of about two years. May also sought to link security and defence to the 'deal' with the EU.

In December 2017, the EU and the UK issued a joint statement (2017) concerning an agreement on the key issues discussed in the first phase of the negotiations. First, the protection of the rights of EU citizens in the UK and UK citizens in the EU was guaranteed to those who exercised free movement rights by the date of withdrawal. Second, both parties reiterated their commitment to avoid a hard border in Ireland. The UK's intention was to achieve this objective through the 'overall EU-UK relationship'. In the absence of agreed solutions, the UK committed to 'maintain full alignment with those rules of the Internal Market and the Customs Union which, now or in the future, support North–South cooperation'. Third, both parties agreed on a methodology to calculate the financial settlement (i.e., the 'divorce bill'), but specific numbers were not spelled out in the document.

The negotiations were deemed to have made sufficient progress to move ahead with the second stage concerning future relations between the UK and the EU. Specifically, the issues to be discussed were: the terms of any free trade/customs agreement between the UK and the EU; and the transition period. Agreement on the latter was agreed in March 2018 such that the transition will last from 'Brexit day' (29 March 2019) till the end of December 2020. The UK has had to concede free movement of people and continued jurisdiction of the ECJ during this period but there will be no 'cliff-edge' on Brexit day regarding UK-EU trade. This agreement followed a speech by May (2018), in which she showed greater realism about UK negotiating objectives. No definitive agreement had been reached at this stage on the thorny issue of the Irish border with Northern Ireland.

Future relations concerning foreign and security policy as well as police cooperation remain under negotiation. The UK government has called for a deep and comprehensive free trade agreement with the EU, building on, but moving beyond, the EU–Canada free trade agreement, namely a 'Canada, plus, plus, plus' agreement, which would include services, especially financial services. Agreement on these issues will take time and goes beyond our time-frame.

Overview of the papers

The first three papers of this collection discuss the implications of Brexit for key EU policies: the single market, finance and immigration. Armstrong (2018) asks to what extent the UK regulatory policy will align with, or diverge from EU policy after Brexit, especially in the medium and long term. He teases out three modes of governance – hierarchy, markets, networks/

community – and argues that the dynamics of regulatory divergence/align-ment between the UK and the EU will be a function of these modes. The paper also considers the mediating influence of the global regulatory context in which both the UK and EU are situated. This paper speaks to the literature on Europeanisation, in general, and the EU's external governance, in particular.

Howarth and Quaglia (2018) analyse the policy developments concerning the Single Market in finance in the context of Brexit. Theoretically, they engage with two bodies of political economy work that make contrasting pre-dictions concerning the Brexit negotiations on finance: the 'battle' amongst member state systems and the transnational financial networks literatures. Empirically, they find limited evidence of the formation of cross-national alli-ances in favour of the UK retaining broad access to the Single Market in finan-cial services. By contrast, the main financial centres in the EU and their national authorities competed to lure financial business away from the United Kingdom. For these reasons the chances of a special deal for the City are slim.

Dennison and Geddes (2018) address the questions of how the debate on 'immigration' influenced Brexit and what are the likely parameters for a post-Brexit regime covering EU citizens and migrants from non-EU member states. They provide a post-functionalist account of migration governance in the context of Brexit, discussing three main components: first, the politicisation of immigration marked by increased issue salience; second, the importance of public opinion preferences rather than those of concentrated interests, such as the business community; and, third, identity-related concerns. They conclude that the referendum exposed the debate about immigration to wider public scrutiny and, by doing so, 'raised more profound questions about the future shape of the British economy and the political model necess-ary to sustain it'.

Schimmelfennig (2018) examines the process of differentiated disinte-gration, meaning the selective reduction of a member state's level and scope of integration, triggered by Brexit. The paper argues that a postfunc-tionalist explanation of differentiated integration also explains the dynamics of disintegration. Thus, Brexit was enabled by integration effects challenging self-determination (immigration), the rise of a Eurosceptic party (UKIP), and the availability of referendums. However, the institutional and material bar-gaining power of states demanding disintegration is considerably lower than of states demanding opt-outs in the context of integration negotiations. Consequently, the expectation is that 'demanders of disintegration moderate their demands and make concessions to the EU' during negotiations.

Krotz and Schild (2018) examine the implications of Brexit for the Franco-German alliance in the EU, and on the two states' relative influence in this bilateral relationship and in the EU at large. In doing so, this contribution also assesses Brexit's implications for the EU's future trajectory. The authors outline three basic future scenarios for the EU: German hegemony; the disintegration of the European project; or a rejuvenated Franco-German relationship as the EU's engine. The outcome will partly depend on the strengthening of Germany's relative standing and France's ability to reform its economy.

Taggart and Szczerbiak (2018) examine the link between the recent EU crises and the development of party-based Euroscepticism across Europe. They identify four main frames through which the EU is contested at the domestic level: economic factors, immigration, democracy/sovereignty and national factors. Their main findings suggest that the sovereign debt crisis in the euro area had powerful a effect in the party systems of those countries most affected by the bailout packages in the euro area periphery and the migration crisis had a strong effect on party politics in the post-communist states of central Europe. By contrast, Brexit has had a very limited impact on national party politics in the EU-27 so far.

Finally, Gamble (2018) explores the pathologies of British politics in the Brexit era. 'Taking back control' and unraveling over 40 years of Europeanisation is more easily said than delivered. However, what is clear is that the EU referendum has brought about a rise of populism, some re-alignment of political parties, de-stabilised the territorial integrity of the UK and raised questions about the future of its foreign policy. Depending on the terms of Brexit, it may bring about significant economic change, too. The referendum vote is therefore having a substantial impact on British politics and political economy.

Conclusion and outlook

The UK's Brexit negotiations come at a challenging time for the EU. The Eurozone and migration crises have not reached definitive resolution. The 'rule of law' challenges in Hungary and Poland pose questions around the EU's core values. The rise of populist Euro-scepticism has arguably made the EU and its policies more politicized than ever before. President Donald Trump is threatening trade sanctions. In different ways he and Russian counterpart President Putin are challenging the view of the international order that the EU represents.

60 years after signature of the Treaty of Rome the European Commission (2017) launched a White Paper on the EU's post-Brexit future. French President Macron has responded and efforts at Franco-German initiatives are under way following Angela Merkel's re-election as chancellor for a fourth term. The UK's departure may remove one semi-detached member from the EU but Brexit is but one of several challenges to EU governance and integration that will be under scrutiny from EU scholars over the coming months and years.

Acknowledgements

We thank the journal editors for their support and advice as well as the referees, who helped strengthen the contributions, and, of course, our contributors. This collection was partly prepared while Lucia Quaglia was a research fellow first at the BIGSSS (University of Bremen) and the Hanse-Wissenschaftskolleg (HWK) and then at the Scuola Normale Superiore (SNS), Florence.

Disclosure statement

No potential conflict of interest was reported by the authors.

References

Armstrong, K. (2018) 'Regulatory alignment and divergence after Brexit', *Journal of European Public Policy*. doi:10.1080/13501763.2018.1467956

Bulmer, S. and James, S. (2018) 'Managing competing projects: unpacking the domestic politics of Brexit', PSA conference paper, 26–28 March.

Cameron, D. (2015) 'EU speech at Bloomberg', 23 January, available at https://www.gov.uk/government/speeches/eu-speech-at-bloomberg

Dennison, J. and Geddes, A. (2018) 'Brexit and the perils of 'Europeanised' immigration', *Journal of European Public Policy*. doi:10.1080/13501763.2018.1467953

European Commission (2017) *White Paper on the Future of Europe: Reflections and Scenarios for the EU27 by 2025*, available at https://ec.europa.eu/commission/sites/beta-political/files/white_paper_on_the_future_of_europe_en.pdf

European Council (2017) *Brexit Guidelines*, 29 April, Brussels, available at http://www.consilium.europa.eu/en/press/press-releases/2017/04/29/euco-brexit-guidelines/

European Parliament (2017) *Resolution on Negotiations with the United Kingdom*, 5 April, Brussels, available at http://www.europarl.europa.eu/sides/getDoc.do?pubRef=-//EP//NONSGML+TA+P8-TA-2017-0102+0+DOC+PDF+V0//EN

EU and UK government (2017) *Joint Report from the Negotiators of the European Union and the United Kingdom Government on Progress during Phase 1 of Negotiations under Article 50 TEU on the United Kingdom's Orderly Withdrawal from the European Union*, 8 December, available at https://ec.europa.eu/commission/sites/beta-political/files/joint_report.pdf

Gamble, A. (2018) 'Taking back control: the political implications of Brexit', *Journal of European Public Policy*. doi:10.1080/13501763.2018.1467952

Howarth, D. and Quaglia, L. (2018) 'Brexit and the battle for financial services', *Journal of European Public Policy*. doi:10.1080/13501763.2018.1467950

Keegan, W., Marsh, D. and Roberts, R. (2017) *Six Days in September: Black Wednesday, Brexit and the Making of Europe*, London: OMFIF.

Krotz, U. and Schild, J. (2018) 'Back to the future? Franco-German bilateralism in Europe's post-Brexit Union', *Journal of European Public Policy*. doi:10.1080/13501763.2018.1467951

May, T. (2017a) 'Speech at Lancaster House', 17 January, available at https://www.gov.uk/government/speeches/the-governments-negotiating-objectives-for-exiting-the-eu-pm-speech

May, T. (2017b) 'Speech in Florence', 22 September, available at https://www.theguardian.com/politics/2017/sep/22/theresa-mays-florence-speech-key-points

May, T. (2018) 'PM speech on our future economic partnership with the European Union', available at https://www.gov.uk/government/speeches/pm-speech-on-our-future-economic-partnership-with-the-european-union

Schimmelfennig, F. (2018) 'Brexit: differentiated disintegration in the European Union', *Journal of European Public Policy*. doi:10.1080/13501763.2018.1467954

Taggart, P and Szczerbiak, A. (2018) 'The effect of Brexit (and other crises) on Euroscepticism in other European states', *Journal of European Public Policy*. doi:10.1080/13501763.2018.1467955

Thatcher, M. (1988) 'The Bruges speech', 20 September, available at https://www.margaretthatcher.org/document/107332

Tratt, J. (1996) *The Macmillan Government and Europe: A Study in the Process of Policy Development*, London: Macmillan.

UK Government (2017) *The United Kingdom's Exit from and New Partnership with the European Union*, February, London, available at https://www.gov.uk/government/uploads/system/uploads/attachment_data/file/589189/The_United_Kingdoms_exit_from_and_partnership_with_the_EU_Print.pdf

Young, H. (1998) *This Blessed Plot: Britain and Europe from Churchill to Blair*, London: Macmillan.

Regulatory alignment and divergence after Brexit

Kenneth A. Armstrong

ABSTRACT

The United Kingdom (UK) has launched the process by which it will terminate its membership of the European Union (EU). A key research question concerns the extent to which UK regulatory policy will align with, or diverge from, EU policy after decades of delegation to, and dependency upon EU rules and regulatory structures. While we ought to expect that UK regulatory policy will continue to align with the EU in the short-term, the scope for future divergence requires further analysis. Whether exiting the EU will lead to regulatory alignment or regulatory divergence is evaluated in light of existing literatures on Europeanisation, in general, and the EU's external governance, in particular. It is contended that the dynamics of alignment/divergence between the UK and EU will be a function of the operation – and interaction – of different modes of governance: hierarchy, markets, coordination and networks/community. However, the study cautions against assumptions that the dynamics of UK regulatory policy post-membership are reducible solely to EU influences. More specifically it contends that the global regulatory context in which both the UK and EU are situated constitutes an important factor that will mediate EU influence over UK policy.

Introduction

The United Kingdom (UK) has triggered the Article 50 TEU process by which it will cease to be a Member State of the European Union (EU). The unprecedented nature of a Member State's departure from the EU and the uncharted territory of the withdrawal process have reinforced a sense of the uniqueness of the Brexit phenomenon. This contribution attempts to move the analysis of Brexit from the back foot of reaction to contemporary events and onto the front foot of hypothesising about future possibilities. The central research questions that underpin the analysis concerns: (1) the extent to which UK regulatory policy will align with, or diverge from, EU policy after decades of delegation to, and dependency upon EU rules and regulatory structures; (2) the continuing influence of the EU on UK policy post-membership.

11

The focal point of the inquiry is upon 'regulatory policy'. As such, other issues pertinent to future EU-UK relations – foreign and security policy cooperation; education, research and innovation; and civil and criminal law cooperation, for example – fall outside its scope. Regulatory policy refers to the range of public interest requirements to which goods and services are required to conform in order to be placed on the European market. The domain of regulatory policy exhibits high – although not uniform – levels of 'Europeanisation' with existing scholarship seeking to understand the mechanisms through which domestic regulatory policy adapts to this Europeanisation (Knill and Lehmkuhl 2002). It is a domain of European cooperation that is also highly 'legalised' in the sense of the scale and depth of legal obligations upon Member States and the delegation of enforcement powers to EU institutions. It is a sphere of EU influence that extends beyond the territorial boundaries of EU Member States. In short, it is a policy domain that is particularly relevant to understanding the dynamics of policy alignment and divergence once the UK ceases to be subject to the discipline of EU membership.

The analysis proceeds in the following steps. It begins by considering the immediate post-membership pressures on regulatory policy under a withdrawal agreement to be negotiated between the UK and the EU (see also Bulmer and Quaglia 2018). Two aspects – a temporally-defined 'transitional period' and a more territorially-located problem concerning the island of Ireland – will be analysed. Looking longer-term and considering the EU and global influences shaping UK regulatory policy, the phenomenon of Brexit is then located within the literature on Europeanisation and the EU's external governance. The aim is to consider whether our understanding of the influence of the EU – typically expressed in terms of the effects of the EU on its members and non-members – can be developed to encompass a former Member State. The core of the analysis conceptualises the dynamics of regulatory alignment/ divergence in respect of the effects of specific modes of governance – hierarchy, competition, coordination and networks/community – that are frequently deployed within the literature. While maintaining that these tools of the Europeanisation literature are helpful ways of explaining regulatory alignment/ divergence, nonetheless, the study also highlights the important of the global regulatory context as a factor mediating future UK-EU regulatory alignment/divergence.

The article 50 withdrawal agreement

A Member State's departure from the EU in terms of Article 50 TEU is facilitated by the negotiation of a withdrawal agreement. Although this functions to unwind a state's membership obligations, it also has the potential to influence the future development of that state's regulatory policies in both the short-term – through a transitional framework – and in the longer-term – because either the resolution of certain issues demands a longer-term solution or simply in anticipation of the definition of that state's future relationship with the EU.

Transitional 'stand-still'

By its own actions and through domestic legislation, the UK intends to ensure that at least at the moment of withdrawal, UK rules will be fully aligned with those of the EU. This 'stand-still' is the aim of a future European Union (Withdrawal) Act. Thereafter, in the short term, what will disciple domestic regulatory policy in the UK will be the effects of any Article 50 withdrawal agreement and the 'transitional arrangements' it adopts.

The EU's negotiating directives specified its requirements for any transitional period:

> Any such transitional arrangements must be clearly defined, limited in time, and subject to effective enforcement mechanisms. Should a time-limited prolongation of Union acquis be considered, this would require existing Union regulatory, budgetary, supervisory, judiciary and enforcement instruments and structures to apply.

To this we also need to add the further European Council guidelines adopted in December 2017 when the EU agreed to move the Article 50 negotiations onto a second phase including negotiating a transitional framework. These guidelines state that the EU will negotiate a transition covering 'the whole of the *acquis*' with the UK also obligated to adopt any new rules during the transitional period.[1]

The European Commission published the draft text of the withdrawal agreement on 28 February 2018, Part Four of which sets out the Commission's view of how transition shall operate.[2] It consists of the continuing application of EU law in the UK during this period, with such Union law producing 'the same legal effects as those which it produces within the Union and its Member States'. Union law is also to be interpreted and applied in accordance with the same methods and general principles as are applicable within the Union. The Common Provisions of the draft agreement also make clear that Union law is to be interpreted 'in conformity with the relevant case of law of the Court of Justice of the European Union handed down before the end of the transition period.'

Temporally, the duration of transition is subject to competing forces. On the one hand, the UK stated a preference for a transition period of around two years but with the proviso that transition should be determined by how long it would take to prepare for the commencement of a new partnership with the EU. By contrast, the negotiating directives for the second phase of Article 50 discussions also identified that transition should not last beyond

2020 and in its draft withdrawal agreement published on 28 February 2018, the European Commission stipulated a fixed end-point for transition of 31 December 2020, coinciding with the end of the multi-annual financial framework. By mid-March 2018 the UK had apparently accepted the EU's somewhat shorter transitional period.

In other words, the effect to be produced during transition is alignment without membership. The discipline of membership is maintained but without the same mechanisms for political representation.

Territorial alignment

Although Brexit is shaped by time (Armstrong 2017), it also has important territorial dimensions. While the UK government is pursuing a policy that will see the UK finally leave the Single Market and the Customs Union, subnational governments like the Scottish Government have suggested that parts of the UK could remain within the Single Market (Skoutaris 2017). However, this sort of territorially differentiated Brexit – which would suggest internal variation in regulatory policy alignment/divergence – has particular salience when it comes to the island of Ireland and the management of the border between Northern Ireland (inside the UK) and Ireland (inside the EU).

The avoidance of a so-called 'hard border' on the island of Ireland is related to the need to avoid regulatory checks on the provision of cross-border goods and services. In part this is about an EU concern to ensure the security of its Single Market. But it is also an issue of the maintenance of the integrity and functioning of the 1998 Belfast 'Good Friday' Agreement that underpins UK-Ireland cooperation on the island of Ireland. The European Commission concluded that regulatory divergence between Northern Ireland and Ireland was the 'biggest single risk' to the forms of cooperation that the Belfast Agreement cemented. However, maintaining regulatory alignment on the island of Ireland risks differentiating the UK's own 'common market' with part of the UK aligned with EU requirements while the rest of the UK might diverge.

After some push-back from the Democratic Unionist Party (DUP) on the original wording, a joint text was agreed during the first phase of Article 50 negotiations that commits the UK to avoiding a hard border. This is to be achieved either 'through the overall EU-UK relationship' or through 'specific solutions to address the unique circumstances on the island of Ireland.'[3] Significantly, however, the joint text committed the UK to a default position should neither an overall future UK-EU relationship nor a specific solution to the problem in Ireland be forthcoming. The joint text provided that the UK 'will maintain full alignment with those rules of the Internal Market and the Customs Union which, now or in the future, support North–South cooperation, the all- island economy and the protection of the 1998 Agreement.' This could have meant maintaining alignment solely in Northern

Ireland. However, the joint text continued that in this default position, the UK 'will ensure that no new regulatory barriers develop between Northern Ireland and the rest of the United Kingdom' unless the Northern Ireland Executive and Assembly 'agree that distinct arrangements are appropriate for Northern Ireland.'

Squaring the circle between regulatory alignment on the island and Ireland and the risk of regulatory divergence between Northern Ireland and the rest of the UK has proved to be a continuing point of contention as evidenced by the Commission's attempt to translate this default position into a Protocol to its draft Withdrawal Agreement. In terms of the draft Protocol, a 'common regulatory area' is to be established between the EU and the UK in respect of Northern Ireland which 'shall constitute an area without internal borders in which the free movement of goods is ensured.' As well as bringing Northern Ireland within the customs territory of the Union, provisions of Union law on goods listed in an Annex would apply 'to and in the United Kingdom in respect of Northern Ireland.' The unpalatability of this outcome for Unionist politicians in Northern Ireland and for UK government ministers may result in either a complete failure to reach an agreement – in which case the issue of alignment/divergence will depend on a different default set of rules governing trade between the UK and the EU in general – or it will focus minds on alternative solutions either within an overarching future UK-EU partnership or a more bespoke negotiated arrangement.

Accordingly, the negotiation of the Withdrawal Agreement highlights both temporal and territorial dimensions of regulatory alignment/divergence. Nonetheless, we need to consider the forces that will shape regulatory alignment/divergence with or without a Withdrawal Agreement. In so doing, the analysis draws on the literatures on Europeanisation and EU external governance to highlight the operation – and interaction – of different modes of governance.

Europeanisation and external governance

If the ambition is to try and mainstream the phenomenon of Brexit within a wider conceptual landscape, then an understanding of the dynamics of regulatory alignment/divergence after EU membership points us towards the literatures on 'Europeanisation' and EU 'external governance'. After all, scholars of Europeanisation typically focus their attention on the influence of the EU on: (1) Member States, (2) potential Member States and (3) non-Member States. Studies of EU external governance specifically highlight the influence of the EU on non-EU states and states that are not, and are unlikely to become, Member States, not least as the pace of EU enlargement declines (Lavenex and Schimmelfennig 2009) or – in the case of the UK – reverses. Brexit creates an opportunity to consider how well the literatures on

Europeanisation and EU external governance manage the novel circum-stances of de-membership.

Nonetheless, in considering the enduring influence of EU regulatory policy on the UK after membership, there is an obvious potential objection to ana-lysing Brexit in terms of Europeanisation at all. After all, de-membership could be considered to be de-Europeanisation. In a rather different context, others have suggested that the term 'diffusion' might be a better way of describing the EU's capacity to exert influence within and beyond its borders (Börzel and Risse 2012). Whatever the semantics, the more significant point is the need to allow any consideration of future EU influence on UK regulatory policy not to become locked in to a purely EU-UK dynamic. In avoiding a kind of 'methodological Europeanism' (Vauchez 2015), the analysis points to the importance of the global context as a mediating factor both as a constraint on the EU and the UK, and as an arena where EU, and potentially, UK influence might be 'uploaded' and diffused.

Scholars of EU external governance are also concerned with the extension or transfer of the EU's rules and policies to non-EU states. Different approaches are taken between those who seek to understand 'integration without mem-bership' by looking at the macro-level of EU/non-EU relations – e.g., the bilat-eral agreements between the EU and Switzerland (Vahl and Grolimund 2006) – and those who contend that it is as the level of the policy sector that greater insights might be gleaned (Lavenex and Schimmelfennig 2009). Recognising that future research will be needed to highlight the varying dynamics of align-ment/divergence in specific policy sectors, the approach adopted here is one that does have regard to the macro-level of future UK-EU relations – in terms of the nature of a future partnership between the UK and the EU – but is also open to explanations of mechanisms of transfer and diffusion beyond formal agreements. Indeed, and drawing on the 'governance' approach of Lavenex and Schimmelfennig (2009), the capacity of a range of 'modes of governance' to generate regulatory alignment or facilitate divergence is analysed. In the section that follows, these modes of governance and their mechanisms of influence and diffusion are explained.

Modes of governance

Studies of EU governance typically highlight the respective operations of 'hier-archy' and 'competition' as dominant modes (Armstrong 2011). Conceptually, hierarchy connotes a coercive form of governance characterised by a rule-based discipline and implementation and enforcement through public insti-tutions. Applied to Brexit, the operation of hierarchy would suggest that UK regulatory alignment/divergence would be a function of the external disci-pline of any future agreement between the UK and the EU or any other instru-ment to which the EU and EU are parties, as well as the institutional apparatus through which such instruments would be implemented and enforced. Governance by competition, on the other hand, examines the influence of market mechanisms in diffusing EU rules and norms beyond the territory of the EU itself. In the context of Brexit, it would be the behaviour of multinational market actors in continuing to comply with EU rules and norms – even in their non-EU market activities – that would constitute a key mechanism of regulatory policy transfer or diffusion. Regulatory competition may ensue with continuing regulatory alignment or novel divergences resulting.

Regulatory alignment or divergence between the UK and the EU may also be explained by reference to additional modes of governance. By contrast with hierarchy, regulatory 'coordination' may operate on the basis of voluntary mutual agreement and negotiation without transferring rule-making to an external body. Administrative structures facilitate this form of horizontal co-ordination. Applied to Brexit, this co-ordinative governance would suggest on-going voluntaristic and negotiated processes of managed alignment or divergence.

A fourth mode of governance can also be considered: governance by 'network' or 'community'. The relevant networks or communities can be public or private actors and the mechanisms of transfer and diffusion are not merely transactional and instrumental, but also entail common socialisation activities and joint knowledge production. When applied to Brexit, the intention is to draw out the epistemic qualities of regulatory policy and the production, application and diffusion of expertise in a range of national, European and international forums and from which regulatory alignment or divergence may emerge.

These modes of governance have variously been deployed specifically in the context of the analysis of the EU's external governance, thereby allowing us to mainstream the analysis of Brexit within existing scholarship on the influence of EU regulatory norms beyond EU borders (Lavenex et al. 2009; Lavenex and Schimmelfennig 2009). Importantly, while these modes are explained separately, it is their interaction which will determine the degree of post-membership regulatory alignment or divergence. In this way, while the extent to which UK policy is required to align with or diverge from EU rules will be a function of the strength and scope of the hierarchical discipline that the UK might be willing to accept under a new partnership with the EU, other modes of governance will influence and act upon the regulatory autonomy the UK seeks to carve out for itself. It will be the constellation of governance modes in any particular policy area that ultimately will influence the degree of alignment or divergence.

Hierarchy

When considering the role of hierarchy in regulatory policy post-EU membership, what is important isn't merely the identification of binding instruments that promote regulatory alignment or inhibit regulatory divergence but rather that these constraints are 'external' to domestic UK politics. This clarification is important not least because a European Union (Withdrawal) Act will enshrine, through national law, the EU *acquis* at the moment that the UK ceases to be a Member State. It is the maintenance of, or divergence from, this legal *status quo* which is the thing that requires explanation.

It is useful to draw a distinction between 'substitute' and 'default' hierarchy *Substitute* hierarchy refers to the idea that the UK could substitute the hierarchy of EU membership with a future agreement between the EU and the UK that will discipline UK regulatory policy one way or another. Here, the UK faces a choice between a 'free trade' discipline that functions against a background of regulatory diversity, or a more intense 'free movement' discipline that mandates alignment and limits local rule-application.

Default hierarchy is the recognition that in the absence of EU membership, and in the absence of a substitute legal framework for cooperation between the EU and the UK – whether the withdrawal agreement or a future UK-EU partnership agreement – default rules and norms can be engaged that exert a disciplining force on UK regulatory policy and on UK-EU economic relations. More precisely, the international trade rules of the World Trade Organisation (WTO) of which both the UK and EU are members would constitute an important example of a default hierarchy.

Substitute hierarchy

The Article 50 process is intended to facilitate the UK's orderly withdrawal from the EU. We have already noted the potential effects of a withdrawal agreement on regulatory alignment. Beyond that agreement it is a new UK-EU partnership agreement that will determine the extent to which UK regulatory policy will be disciplined by a substitute hierarchy.

If the UK opted to frame that new relationship in terms of rejoining the European Free Trade Association and maintaining access to the Single Market through the European Economic Area (EEA) Agreement, then the disciplinary effects of a substitute hierarchy would be very clear. The EEA agreement replicates the free movement provisions of the TFEU that inhibit contracting parties from introducing new measures that would create obstacles to trade. This is intended to limit regulatory divergence. Regulatory alignment (or 'homogeneity') is also secured through the pre-commitment of the participating EFTA states to the implementation of new EU acts incorporated into the EEA Agreement by the EEA Joint Committee. As a model of substitute hierarchy, it would come closest to replicating the existing free movement discipline of EU membership. It would be particularly relevant in respect of regulatory alignment on the island of Ireland and, notwithstanding that agriculture and fisheries are largely outside of the EEA Agreement, food safety, veterinary, sanitary and phytosanitary matters form part of the Food Package Law under the EEA Agreement and would be applicable in respect of cross-border trade in food and livestock.

However, the UK Government has repeatedly stated that it does not favour the EFTA/EEA option precisely because it believes it would oblige the UK to follow EU rules while having no say in EU decision-making processes. The UK's decision to leave the Single Market and the Customs Union is to interpret the 2016 referendum result as meaning that control over domestic regulatory policy is valued more highly than continuing access to the Single Market. Accordingly, the UK will seek some form of free trade agreement that will afford it greater regulatory autonomy. This has consequences both in terms of the scope and nature of the discipline thereby created.

In terms of scope, the focus of EU free trade agreements is principally on goods. The battle for the UK will be to have services included – particularly financial services – to secure continuing market access. In respect of the nature of the discipline that such agreements exert, they incorporate a free trade discipline in which regulatory autonomy and local regulation is the default position. Goods will comply with the local rules in each and every market on which they are placed: 'national treatment'. It is precisely this sort of regulatory diversity that EU membership challenges through a more intense free movement discipline that encourages regulatory harmonisation and discourages the multiple application of local rules.

Despite much talk about the UK following Canada, Norway, Switzerland or Ukraine trade models, there is, therefore, a more binary choice between more extensive market access – with the *quid pro quo* being acceptance of a con-straining free movement discipline – or receiving more limited market access but with greater regulatory autonomy.

Default hierarchy

Both the EU and the UK are members of the WTO. If the UK were to leave the EU without any withdrawal agreement and with no trade deal in place, then economic relations between the EU and UK would fall back onto WTO terms. WTO law on goods and services operates under distinct legal instruments: the General Agreement on Tariffs and Trade (GATT) and the General Agreement on Trade in Services (GATS). There are also other specific instruments on Intellectual Property (TRIPS), Technical Barriers to Trade (TBT) and Sanitary and Phytosanitary measures (SPS).

The WTO lacks the same legislative capacity as the EU to harmonise rules. This then leaves regulatory powers in the hand of its members and as described already, market access is sought on the basis of 'national treatment'. Under WTO law, local regulations can be challenged as discriminatory and unduly trade restrictive having regard to their legitimate regulatory objective.

It is then for member countries to demonstrate the 'necessity' of their measures despite their trade-restrictive effects. While analogous to the proportionality test that is a central part of EU free movement legal discipline, it needs to be recalled that the strictness of the EU's proportionality analysis is a function of its objective of creating a Single Market and a regulatory level-playing field in an integrating EU. By contrast, the necessity test in WTO law starts from a background of managing regulatory diversity and regulatory autonomy among sovereign states (Cottier and Oesch 2011).

Future exercises of UK regulatory policy competence would – vis-à-vis other WTO members including the EU – be subject to this type of legal discipline. In general, this would give the EU the power to challenge future and divergent exercises of UK regulatory powers (and vice versa) insofar as they were alleged to be discriminatory or unduly trade restrictive having regard to their policy objective. The question would then be whether the UK could justify the necessity of its rules by reference to exceptions recognised under the specific WTO agreements.

Although the WTO lacks the EU's legislative capacity for harmonisation, member countries are expected to base their regulations on harmonised international standards where they exist. Nonetheless, this is not an absolute obligation and still gives WTO members flexibility (Scott 2009). It is also qualitatively very different from the coerced compliance with harmonised EU rules that forms a core aspect of EU Single Market law and which sees regulatory authority transferred from the nation state to the EU itself.

Given the weaker discipline exerted by free trade rules – whether as a substitute or default hierarchy – a space emerges for greater post-EU membership regulatory autonomy. What now needs to be considered is whether the operation of other modes of governance is likely to give rise to regulatory alignment or divergence.

Competition

During the UK's EU membership, UK firms accessing the Single Market have complied with EU regulatory requirements. Provided UK and EU rules remain as they are at the point of the UK's departure from the EU, then for UK-based firms with long exposure to the regulatory requirements of EU harmonised rules, this is not likely to be problematic in that the costs of compliance with EU rules are already factored in. Provided there are no other impediments to market access, then keeping things the same would clearly suit certain sectors of the UK economy. However, for some UK firms exposed to the regulatory requirements of harmonised EU rules but without any or significant cross-border economic activities, the promise of Brexit might be that UK rules can, and should, diverge. The key issue explored here is whether EU and UK rules could diverge because (1) the UK wants less stringent requirements than currently pertain in the EU; (2) the EU seeks new stricter standards; or (3) the UK wants to depart from its domesticated EU regulatory *acquis* and adopt requirements more stringent than those in the EU. To what extent does regulatory competition inhibit such divergences?

The UK might consider adopting less stringent regulations particularly to respond to small businesses with no or little exposure to the EU Single Market. However, larger firms with significant cross-border activities may consider it to be in their interest to continue to comply with EU rules. As the concept of the 'Brussels Effect' highlights, this continued compliance with Single Market rules may extend beyond the Single Market activities of non-EU firms to include their UK operations insofar as compliance with EU norms meets and exceeds less stringent UK regulatory demands.

Bradford describes 'the Brussels Effect' as 'unilateral regulatory globalisation', meaning the extension of EU regulatory norms and practices beyond the EU territory but outside of the structures and institutions of hierarchical public rule-making (Bradford 2012). More specifically, it is the behaviour of market actors that drives this externalisation of EU regulatory policy. Bradford highlights the manner in which non-EU firms with European and global market presence comply with regulatory requirements in the EU – including higher standards – to avoid the additional costs of compliance with multiple rules and to gain the economies of scale achieved by manufacturing towards one set of requirements. Applied to Brexit, this would entail UK firms with cross-border economic activities maintaining their compliance with existing EU Single Market rules including in their UK operations insofar as the EU requirements were not inconsistent with UK rules. Meanwhile, UK firms operating solely in the UK market could opt to comply with less stringent UK rules. In this way, different operators within the UK could simply make different regulatory-compliance choices depending upon the location and scale of their market operations.

If the EU were to introduce more stringent regulatory requirements than existed during the UK's membership, it is conceivable that the EU could face challenges if such changes were regarded as discriminatory or unjustifiably trade restrictive. But absent that sort of complaint, then again the Brussels Effect would suggest that UK firms could continue to comply with more stringent EU requirements provided the benefits of access to the larger Single Market outweighed any additional costs of compliance. Importantly and for the same reasons already given, UK firms would want their compliance with high EU standards to also permit them to operate in the UK market and indeed other non-EU markets to which UK companies might have – or under any new UK trade deals, obtain – market access. In this way, EU regulatory influence would be diffused beyond its own territory through the market behaviour of UK economic actors.

The capacity for the UK to depart from its domesticated EU regulatory *acquis* by enacting more stringent requirements, by contrast, would seem to be much more limited. Given that it would impact on all firms operating within its territory it would likely be resisted by those smaller UK firms for whom Brexit was an opportunity to lighten regulatory burdens and for larger UK-based companies facing increased regulatory compliance costs. EU-based companies would need to consider whether the benefits of access to the UK market outweighed additional compliance costs and whether to pressure the EU to challenge any discriminatory or unjustifiably trade restrictive effects of any changes.

In thinking about the potential effects of regulatory competition between the UK and EU it is important not to treat this as a static closed system. Both the UK and the EU will face competitive influences at a global level. Indeed, the issue for the UK and the EU may be how best to seek to influence the global regulatory environment in order to manage regulatory competition.

As Smith suggests, in order to minimise the risk that Single Market integration might come at the expense of global competitiveness, the EU has a strong incentive to promote a wider global alignment around is own regulatory strategies (Smith 2010). Indeed for Damro, the EU's 'market power' lies in the capacity of the EU to externalise its internal policies including its regulatory measures (Damro 2012, 2015). As he argues (Damro 2015), an externalisation of regulatory power

> occurs when the institutions and actors of the EU attempt to get other actors to adhere to a level of regulation similar to that in effect in the European single market or to behave in a way that generally satisfies or conforms to the EU's market-related policies and regulatory measures.

Like Bradford, Damro's conceptualisation of the external reach of EU regulatory norms depends on similar scope conditions including market size, institutional factors – and that would include the EU's institutional regulatory capacity – and interest contestation – which includes the interests of market actors but extends more broadly to encompass wider societal interests. The more that the EU succeeds in setting global regulatory requirements the more that compliance with international regulatory norms is in fact alignment with EU regulatory policy.

Nonetheless, the EU's record in uploading its regulatory preferences to the global market is far from uniform (Newman and Posner 2015; Young 2015). Newman and Posner suggest a likely differentiation across policy areas which recognises that the EU's external influence is neither static nor uniform. For them, the global regulatory context matters and is likely to give rise to the pursuit of different strategies from norm exportation and first-mover agenda-setting strategies to mutual recognition and coalition-building.

Young suggests that the EU's external influence depends upon whether regulatory policy exportation occurs through policy diffusion – and this includes via regulatory competition incentivising non-EU regulators to 'trade up' to stricter EU requirements (Vogel 1997) – or through regulatory co-operation – including via rule-mediated international fora. Young argues that the scope conditions for EU influence in terms of direct regulatory competition are often simply extended to the different contexts of regulatory cooperation where other factors come into play and which give rise to more uneven patterns of EU influence. These factors include things like the formal rule-making processes, the extent and nature of EU external legal competence, and the ability of the EU to adopt a coherent and consistent position. For example, and using the example of international financial regulation following on from the financial crisis a decade ago, Quaglia highlights a variegated pattern of EU influence in international regulatory fora even within the field of financial services (Quaglia 2014). Nonetheless, the presence of fora to adopt international regulatory rules or standards creates an opportunity to strive and compete for influence over the contents of those norms and their alignment with either national or regional regulatory preferences.

In the context of Brexit the question is whether the UK can escape the dynamics of direct regulatory competition with the EU and instead aspire to be a regulatory power in its own right, consistent with its wider ambition to forge 'Global Britain' in trade and economic terms. While the literature might be more pessimistic about the UK's future capacity to win a straight regulatory competition fight with the EU, there may be spaces within structures of international regulatory cooperation where the UK could seek to exert influence and manage risks from regulatory competition. The challenge for the UK is whether it can organise expertise and develop either, credible alternative models of regulation (in areas where EU regulatory policy may have underperformed) or, novel regulatory responses not least where technological change is driving significant change in, or indeed, creating new, markets. But what the literature would suggest is that we ought to expect significant variation across, and even within, policy fields.

Managed co-ordination

Co-ordination as a mode of EU governance can take different forms and as intimated in the previous section may extend beyond Europe into international fora. It finds particular expression through the mechanism of 'mutual recognition' as a means of managing regulatory diversity by a co-ordinated search for 'equivalence' (Armstrong 2002).

As an alternative to the hierarchical discipline of harmonisation or competition-generating 'national treatment' (Schmidt 2007), mutual recognition can take a variety of forms. At one extreme, mutual recognition may be mandated insofar as EU legislation demands Member States to recognise and give effect to regulatory activities carried out in other Member States. This occurs in respect of the mutual recognition of certain professional qualifications. Even if legislation has not pre-determined the equivalence between different regimes, EU rules can instead formalise a process of authorisation by which an equivalence is accepted. It is through 'equivalence decisions' that the EU accepts the supervisory functions of non-EU countries in allowing their firms to offer financial services within the EU (see Howarth and Quaglia (2018)). The particular value of both legislated mutual recognition and authorised mutual recognition is that it produces EU legal acts with binding and certain outcomes.

Nonetheless, mutual recognition also has a more dynamic potential to mediate between divergent regimes in a form of decentralised horizontal co-ordination. Through a more active process of discovery, regulators can seek to determine whether to permit cross-border market access on the basis of compliance with functionally equivalent requirements. To the extent that such activities are carried out, they are typically at an administrative level albeit with the possibility of challenging non-recognition decisions through courts.

It seems clear from the UK Prime Minister's Mansion House speech on 2 March 2018 setting out her ambitions for a new relationship with the EU, that the UK believes it can manage future regulatory diversity through 'a comprehensive system of mutual recognition.'[4] Nonetheless, the capacity of this mode of governance to work is not unrelated to the choice of discipline discussed earlier. That is to say, that while mutual recognition is an aspect of modern EU free trade deals, it takes a particular form. It permits recognition of testing and certification rather than offering access to the EU market by compliance with the rules of origin. In other words, it entails recognition of conformity assessment of compliance with EU substantive rules. By contrast, acceptance of the discipline of the Single Market – participation in the rules and structures which aim to maximise market access – and the mutual trust that it implies, opens up the possibility for the operation of more active substantive mutual recognition. The UK seems to want this latter type of mutual recognition but with the lesser discipline of a free trade arrangement.

In short, while it is clear that the management of regulatory divergence through horizontal co-ordination and active mutual recognition is an ambition for the UK, it is not obvious that the legal and institutional preconditions which make that possible would exist. Indeed, it might even be considered to be a more ambitious form of mutual recognition than is achieved in practice among EU Member States.

Networks and communities

Governance by networks and communities has a more heterogeneous quality when compared to other modes of governance. After all, there is a broad scope to give organised expression to this mode of governance in the form of working groups, committees, bodies and agencies, formal and informal networks. These institutional forms might also be considered to be the mere handmaidens of the hierarchy of public rule-making, operating to ensure the effective implementation and enforcement of regulatory frameworks.

Nonetheless, there are good reasons for thinking about networks and communities as a mode of governance and as a source of influence on domestic regulatory policymaking (Maggetti and Gilardi 2011). Particularly given regulatory policy's constant demands for information, expertise and science the practice of regulation blurs the boundaries between rule-promulgation and rule-implementation (Scott 2011). Regulators rely upon epistemic networks and knowledge communities to inform the content and application of regulatory frameworks. Arguably, this is an aspect of Brexit that has attracted insufficient attention. One significant dimension lies in considering the degree to which UK regulatory bodies will have access to, or engagement with, specifically EU-created or EU-oriented regulatory networks and communities. These include agency and network structures in areas such as energy, telecoms, railways, medicines, chemicals and competition regulation (Coen and Thatcher 2008). This will likely turn on what sort of substitute hierarchy the UK agrees with the EU by way of a future relationship. Whatever the formal legal mechanism, keeping UK regulators close to EU structures would be an important driver of continuing regulatory convergence.

Even without direct organisational participation in EU structures, there may still be a diffusion of expertise and world-views through less formal knowledge-exchange processes. These 'cognitive inputs' into UK policymaking – a feature of the Europeanization of regulatory policy during EU membership (Knill and Lehmkuhl 2002) – may continue to persist after membership. That exchange could take place simply through transparency in the EU's regulatory activities – the routine production of working documents, reports and guidance – or through meetings, conferences and other 'peer'-related gatherings of regulators working in particular policy fields. For example, in an area like competition law, not only are there formal networks of competition regulators (Maher 2002), it is a domain where expertise is routinely shared through publications and conferences and less formal meetings. It is the means and mechanisms by which professional regulators constitute themselves as a network and community and find avenues for knowledge-exchange that may still motivate regulatory alignment between the EU and the UK.

Although the argument has focused on the bureaucratic level of expertise, it is also worth highlighting that there is also another community that engages and interacts with the expertise and knowledge that underpins EU regulatory norms: lawyers and judges. The Withdrawal Agreement and domestic UK legislation is set to provide guidance to UK courts as to the extent to which they are entitled or mandated to give interpretations of domestic EU-derived law in ways that are consistent with EU law and with judgments of EU courts. But even in the absence of such legal instructions, the very nature and specificity of the regulatory regimes and practices of interpretation and application by regulators and courts alike, seems more likely to tend towards maintaining regulatory convergence than divergence. While it is often said that UK courts are inclined towards more literal than purposive interpretations of statutes, courts cannot help but engage with the functional demands of regulatory systems including shared understandings of the purposes of regulatory intervention. None of which inhibits future UK governments from steering domestic policy in another direction with the expectation that courts will follow suit. The point, however, is that UK judges will look for specific instructions that policy divergence is both permitted and mandated.

Any analysis of the influence of networks and communities on future EU-UK regulatory alignment/divergence has to embrace two other important dimensions. The first is the need to look beyond the regional level to the dynamics of global regulatory standard-setting. As highlighted previously, the more that regulation in inspired by global standards the more that the EU and UK ought to align around those standards. 'Market power' in influencing those standards isn't just a matter of political influence but also the capacity to bring knowledge and expertise to an understanding of what sort of problems regulators face and how they might be tackled.

The other dimension is where standard-setting – regional or international – is driven not by public rule makers but by private actors. Organised structures of private governance also perform important regulatory functions whether on their own or in collaboration with public regulators (Scott et al. 2011). This moves private actors beyond the traditional domain of the market and into a sphere of self-organising or collaborative decision-making that can facilitate market access while delivering regulatory objectives.

A key example of this at both European and international level is the production of technical standards. At a European level, bodies like CEN, CENELEC and ETSI produce harmonised European technical standards. Production of standards and compliance with standards is a voluntary decision of private actors (albeit that it can be harnessed towards showing conformity to mandatory technical regulations). So regardless of whether UK regulators retain access to EU regulatory structures, UK firms and UK bodies like the British Standards Institute will retain access to these private communities of standards-setters. Where harmonised standards exist, regulatory alignment around the use of these standards ought to be maintained even after the UK's withdrawal from the EU.

The concept of network or community governance is often better at describing particular institutional forms of governance (Levi-Faur 2011), or institutionalised patterns of interest mediation between public and private actors (Börzel 2011) rather than identifying a distinctive 'mode'. Nonetheless, the analysis presented here suggests that if we are to understand the dynamics of regulatory alignment/divergence post-EU membership, we need to think carefully about how networks and communities organise expertise, generate knowledge and influence the diffusion of regulatory norms and standards.

Conclusions

As the UK continues along a path that will see it leave the European Union, it becomes increasingly necessary to look beyond the immediate politics of the referendum and the apparent exceptionalism of Brexit. In particular, it is important to build on existing scholarship to explore post-membership EU influences on UK domestic regulatory policy and the conditions under which EU-UK regulatory alignment or divergence will take place.

In the short term, the adoption of a transitional framework combined with domestic incorporation of the EU regulatory *acquis* will secure regulatory alignment. Moreover, in starting from a position of convergence, regulatory divergence will be slow to occur. Future regulatory alignment/divergence will be a function of the operation and interaction of different modes of governance: hierarchy, competition, co-ordination networks and community. What will matter is how these modes combine and interact in specific policy areas. In that respect the dynamics of alignment and divergence will be accompanied by variation.

The orthodoxy from the Europeanization and EU external governance literature would tend to suggest that the UK will remain heavily influenced by the EU in the years following EU membership. But in a rapidly changing global economic and regulatory context, it will be important to be sensitive to the full range of push and pull factors that will shape the trajectory of UK regulatory policy. Indeed, the challenge for the UK may lie in working out how best to extend regulatory influence beyond its own territory in much the same way as the EU has sought to do. In this respect, future regulatory alignment or divergence between the UK and the EU is also a litmus test for whether global influence is better sought by states going it alone or by forming collaborative trade blocs.

Notes

1. EUCO XT 20011/17 (15.12.2017).
2. TF50 (2018) 33 (28.2.2017)
3. TF50 (2017) 19 (8.12.2017), para 49.
4. https://www.gov.uk/government/speeches/pm-speech-on-our-future-economic-partnership-with-the-european-union

Acknowledgements

The author would like to thank Simon Bulmer and Lucia Quaglia for their invitation to contribute to this special issue and for their advice and support throughout the writing and editorial process. The author is also extremely grateful to the anonymous reviewers for the care with which they read and commented on earlier drafts. This article is an early attempt to develop a framework for analysis of future regulatory alignment/divergence issues in the context of Brexit. A more detailed empirical analysis will be pursued under the auspices of a Leverhulme Trust Major Research Fellowship running from 2018–21. Comments to the author are very welcome and can be sent to kaa40@cam.ac.uk.

Disclosure statement

No potential conflict of interest was reported by the author.

References

Armstrong, K.A. (2002) 'Mutual recognition', in J. Scott and G. de Búrca (eds.), *The Law of the Single European Market: Unpacking the Premises*, Oxford: Hart Publishing, pp. 225–267.

Armstrong, K.A. (2011) 'The character of EU law and governance: from "Community Method" to new modes of governance', *Current Legal Problems* 63: 179–214.

Armstrong, K.A. (2017) *Brexit Time - Leaving the EU: Why, How and When?*, Cambridge: Cambridge University Press.

Börzel, T.A. (2011) 'Networks: reified metaphor or governance panacea?', *Public Administration* 89(1): 49–63.

Börzel, T.A. and Risse, T. (2012) 'From Europeanisation to diffusion: introduction', *West European Politics* 35(1): 1–19.

Bradford, A. (2012) 'The Brussels effect', *Northwestern University Law Review* 107(1): 1–67.

Bulmer, S. and Quaglia, L. (2018) 'Introduction', *Journal of European Public Policy* 25(8).

Coen, D. and Thatcher, M. (2008) 'Network governance and multi-level delegation: european networks of regulatory agencies', *Journal of Public Policy* 28(1): 49–71.

Cottier, T. and Oesch, M. (2011) 'Direct and indirect discrimination in WTO law and EU law', *NCCR Trade Regulation Working Paper 2011/16*.

Damro, C. (2012) 'Market power Europe', *Journal of European Public Policy* 19(5): 682–99.

Damro, C. (2015) 'Market power Europe: exploring a dynamic conceptual framework', *Journal of European Public Policy* 22(9): 1336–54.

Howarth, D. and Quaglia, L. (2018) 'Brexit and the battle for financial services', *Journal of European Public Policy* 25(8).

Knill, C. and Lehmkuhl, D. (2002) 'The national impact of European Union regulatory policy: Three Europeanization mechanisms', *European Journal of Political Research* 41(2): 255–80.

Lavenex, S., Lehmkuhl, D. and Wichmann, N. (2009) 'Modes of external governance: a cross-national and cross-sectoral comparison', *Journal of European Public Policy* 16 (6): 813–33.

Lavenex, S. and Schimmelfennig, F. (2009) 'EU rules beyond EU borders: theorizing external governance in European politics', *Journal of European Public Policy* 16(6): 791–812.

Levi-Faur, D. (2011) 'Regulatory networks and regulatory agencification: towards a single European regulatory space', *Journal of European Public Policy* 18(6): 810–29.

Maggetti, M. and Gilardi, F. (2011) 'The policy-making structure of European regulatory networks and the domestic adoption of standards', *Journal of European Public Policy* 18(6): 830–47.

Maher, I. (2002) 'Competition law in the international domain: networks as a new form of governance', *Journal of Law and Society* 29(1): 111–36.

Newman, A.L. and Posner, E. (2015) 'Putting the EU in its place: policy strategies and the global regulatory context', *Journal of European Public Policy* 22(9): 1316–35.

Quaglia, L. (2014) 'The sources of European Union influence in international financial regulatory fora', *Journal of European Public Policy* 21(3): 327–45.

Scott, C., Cafaggi, F. and Senden, L. (2011) *The Challenge of Transnational Private Regulation: Conceptual and Constitutional Debates*, Oxford: Wiley-Blackwell.

Scott, J. (2009) *The WTO Agreement on Sanitary and Phytosanitary Measures: A Commentary*, Oxford: Oxford University Press.

Scott, J. (2011) 'In legal limbo: post-legislative guidance as a challenge for European administrative law', *Common Market Law Review* 48(2): 329–55.

Schmidt, S.K. (2007) 'Mutual recognition as a new mode of governance', *Journal of European Public Policy* 14(5): 667–81.

Skoutaris, N. (2017) 'Territorial differentiation in EU law: can Scotland and Northern Ireland remain in the EU and/or the single market?', *Cambridge Yearbook of European Legal Studies* 19: 287–310.

Smith, M.P. (2010) 'Single market, global competition: regulating the european market in a global economy', *Journal of European Public Policy* 17(7): 936–53.

Vauchez, A. (2015) 'Methodological Europeanism at the cradle: eur-lex, the acquis and the making of Europe's cognitive equipment', *Journal of European Integration* 37(2): 193–210.

Vahl, M. and Grolimund, N. (2006) *Integration Without Membership: Switzerland's Bilateral Agreements with the European Union*, Brussels: Centre for European Policy Studies.

Vogel, D. (1997) 'Trading up and governing across: transnational governance and environmental protection', *Journal of European Public Policy* 4(4): 556–71.

Young, A.R. (2015) 'The European Union as a global regulator? Context and comparison', *Journal of European Public Policy* 22(9): 1233–52.

Brexit and the battle for financial services

David Howarth and Lucia Quaglia

ABSTRACT
This paper analyses the policy developments concerning the Single Market in finance in the context of Brexit. Theoretically, we engage with two bodies of work that make contrasting predictions on European financial market integration and the development of European Union (EU) policies on financial regulation: one focused upon a neo-mercantilist 'battle' amongst member states and the other stressing the importance of transnational financial networks (or coalitions). Empirically, we find limited evidence of the formation of cross-national alliances in favour of the United Kingdom (UK) retaining broad access to the EU Single Market in financial services, the presence of which would have aligned with the expectations of analyses focused upon transnational networks. By contrast, the main financial centres in the EU27 and their national authorities competed to lure financial business away from the UK – what we explain in terms of a 'battle' amongst member states and their national financial centres.

Introduction

The United Kingdom (UK) is the world's largest exporter of financial services and approximately one third of that export goes to the European Union (EU). Hence, the decision of the UK government to leave the EU triggered widespread concern on the future of the financial sector, both in the UK and in the EU. Key issues concerned both the impact of Brexit on the financial sector in the UK and in the EU27; and the political bargaining power that this would give to the UK and the EU during the Brexit negotiations. The academic literature on the political economy of finance and the politics of financial regulation in the EU makes contrasting predictions concerning these key issues. A neo-mercantilist state-centric body of academic work that emphasizes the competition amongst the member states and their financial centres in the EU (Fioretos 2010; Howarth and Quaglia 2013; Story and Walters 1997) would predict that the limitation of access to the Single Market following Brexit would encourage the relocation of financial activities to other EU financial centres, which would therefore seek pro-actively to lure business from London. More generally, this body of work predicts that any piece of EU financial regulation that potentially has significant distributive conse- quences – largely but not entirely due to the make-up of different national financial systems – will result in a 'battle' amongst member states. By contrast, a second body of academic work that draws from the literature on transna- tional finance (Macartney 2010; Mügge 2010; Van Apeldoorn 2002) and the new interdependence (Farrell and Newman 2016; Newman and Posner 2016) would predict that cross-national alliances would mobilize in favour of the UK retaining broad access to the Single Market.

In this paper, we ask whether Brexit triggered a 'battle for finance' amongst the member states and their financial centres to attract business from the UK, or whether cross-border coalitions mobilised with a view to securing as much market access as possible and why this was the case. This issue is of immense economic and political significance given the potential impact of Brexit nego- tiation outcomes on the development of a key economic sector – finance – in the UK and the EU. An examination of this issue also provides a valuable opportunity to speak to the broader academic debate on the relative impor- tance of state-centric explanations versus transnational networks to the devel- opment of financial governance in the EU and elsewhere.

This paper is structured as follows. We first review the literature on the poli- tics and political economy of financial market integration in the EU. We then map the preferences and the mobilization of various parts of the financial industry in the UK, as well as the positions to date (April 2018) of the UK auth- orities during the Brexit negotiations on finance. We do the same with refer- ence to the other two main EU member states, namely Germany and France which, respectively, had the second and third largest financial sectors in the EU and, in Frankfurt and Paris, respectively, had the third and second largest financial centres in the EU by total assets. These were also the most influential member states in the context of Brexit negotiations (Krotz and Schild 2018). We recognize that a number of other second-tier EU27 financial centres and member states with significant financial sectors had the potential to gain from Brexit – notably Dublin (Ireland), Brussels (Belgium), Amsterdam (the Netherlands) and Luxembourg. However, given limited space we do not focus upon these. Empirical material was gathered though a systematic survey of press coverage and policy documents, as well as semi-structured interviews with representatives of EU-headquartered banks, EU-based banking associ- ations, business associations, and national government officials responsible for financial affairs.

Our findings suggest that the main financial centres in the EU and their national authorities competed to lure financial business away from the UK, in line with the 'battle' amongst member states approach. In contrast, the for- mation and mobilization of cross-national alliances in favour of the UK retaining broad access to the Single Market in financial services mostly failed to materialize, contrary to the expectations of the transnational finance litera- ture and the new interdependence approach. The main caveat of our analysis is that the Brexit negotiations are ongoing at the time of writing. Nonetheless, a broadly convincing argument on the positioning of financial interests and national authorities can be already presented.

State of the art on the political economy of European financial market integration

We consider two alternative explanations, which are rooted in the literature on the politics and political economy of EU financial integration. The first explanation is mostly state-centric and focuses on the competition amongst member states and their financial centres in order to attract financial business in the Single Market. The early literature on the 'battle of the systems' (Story and Walter 1997) argues that national authorities seek to promote EU financial integration in a way that protects their national varieties of financial capital- ism. Although national financial systems have partly converged across the EU over time, distinctive features remain. Hence, a more recent version of this literature points out the competition amongst member states to ensure that EU financial regulation does not penalize their financial industry or impor- tant parts of it, such as hedge funds in the UK (Fioretos 2010), or savings banks in Germany (Howarth and Quaglia 2013). Moreover, the member states might undertake domestic reforms that make their financial centres more attractive (for example, Lütz 1998).

According to this approach, in the context of Brexit, we would expect a neo-mercantilist 'battle' for finance between the UK-based financial industry, notably the City of London, and other EU financial centres, jostling for position to attract business from London, with support from their respective local and national authorities. More specifically, one would expect attempts by the EU (and the main member states therein) to restrict the ability of UK-based firms to provide a range of financial services, including clearing, to the rest of the EU because this would encourage the relocation of these financial activities to the main EU27 financial centres.

Second, one would expect that each financial centre would seek to play to its comparative advantages because what it could gain from Brexit in terms of new financial operations depended largely on the national variety of financial capitalism. Consequently, Germany and France would be well positioned to attract business in banking, as they would have – post-Brexit – respectively, the first and second largest banking sectors by total assets in the EU, with the concentration of sophisticated investment banking activities in Frankfurt and Paris (Howarth 2013). Furthermore, Paris and to a lesser extent Frankfurt were well-positioned to attract the clearing of euro denominated derivatives in case the EU – and more specifically the euro area and the ECB – adopted restrictions on euro clearing.

However, continental financial centres were far less appealing than London in most of these financial services for a number of reasons: notably, the concentration of expertise in London, the UK's comparatively light-touch regulatory framework, advantages linked to the use of English common law, and the country's established financial infrastructure (see Bank of England 2015; Batsaikhan et al. 2017). Brexit created an incentive for the national authorities to attempt to woo business from London by making certain features of the national financial system – notably regulation – and related areas – notably tax policy – more appealing to UK-based financial services. Hence, one would expect some domestic reforms in this direction.

The alterative explanation examined in this paper draws on the literature on transnational finance (Graz and Noelke 2008; Macartney 2010; Mügge 2010; Tsingou 2008), which considers EU financial integration as a reflection of the interests of big financial companies, first and foremost British, French and German banks, whose businesses had become pan-European (see also Van Apeldoorn 2002) and the literature on 'new interdependence' (Farrell and Newman 2016, 2017; Newman and Posner 2016), which examines the formation of cross-border coalitions brought together by mutual interdependence. For example, in the EU context, Posner (2009) and Quaglia (2010) consider the role of transnational networks (or coalitions) in the making of EU financial regulation over the last two decades.

These two bodies of work pay attention to the mobilization of transnational networks (coalitions) of private and public actors seeking to protect and expand cross border flows. For example, Farrell and Newman (2015) explain how transnational coalitions generated by financial interdependence were instrumental in settling transatlantic regulatory disputes in finance. According to this literature, in the context of Brexit, we would expect financial firms engaged in cross-border business in the UK and the EU27 to mobilize because their profits would be significantly affected by reduced market access. Hence, we would expect the formation of a transnational coalition lobbying on both sides of the Channel with a view to preserving as much as possible the current level of market access between the UK and the EU27, securing a special deal for finance.

We would also expect that this industry coalition would be spearheaded by the main EU-level lobby groups representing the interests of cross-border finance. Moreover, since London is the fulcrum for the more internationally-oriented financial firms in Europe, we would expect that these UK-based financial associations would seek to mobilize their counterparts in the EU27 and that the UK public authorities would also seek to elicit the involvement of the EU27 based financial industry and national governments with a view to preserving as much market access as possible.[1]

The UK and the Single Market in finance

After the referendum, the priority for the bulk of the UK-based financial industry was to preserve membership of and full access to the Single Market. It soon became clear that a European Economic Area (EEA) style arrangement post-Brexit was not feasible for the UK government because of its commitment to ending free movement of labour (Bulmer and Quaglia 2018). As its main alternative, the UK-based financial industry favoured a special deal for finance which, however, was not politically feasible for the EU Commission and several member states, which insisted publicly on maintaining all four freedoms of the internal market or none (Armstrong 2018). Hence, the British financial industry called for the preservation of as much market access as possible (The CityUK 2016a, 2016b). The Conservative government's 'Brexit White Paper' of February 2017 (UK government 2017) made clear that the UK would not seek Single Market membership after Brexit. Nonetheless, the White Paper also highlighted 'a legitimate interest in mutual cooperation arrangements that recognize the interconnectedness of markets' (p. 42) in finance.

Once the UK government outlined its plan for a hard Brexit in early 2017, the UK-based financial industry recognized that it would not be able to preserve the EU passport. Hence, most British financial services campaigned in favour of an extensive use of equivalence,[2] in order to secure as much access as possible to the Single Market (see, for example, Ford 2017). The City also asked for a long transition period out of the Single Market (The CityUK 2016a, 2016b). The strategy adopted by the UK-based financial industry was to point out that it provided a variety of services to 'customers' across Europe and that those services were necessary and could not be easily switched to other locations. Moreover, the City argued that restrictions imposed on British financial services to access the Single Market or to clear euro denominated assets would result in higher costs and more risks for customers across the EU.

According to the 'battle' amongst member states approach, given the economic strength of the financial industry in the UK, one would have expected that the UK government would try to protect this sector by securing continued broad access to the Single Market after Brexit. However, the UK government downplayed the preferences of the UK-based financial industry. Three clarifications regarding the limited influence of the financial industry in the UK must be made. First, the negotiations on finance were part of a broader set of negotiations, whereby it would have been politically difficult for the UK government to grant finance a special status. Second, there were divisions within the UK government, whereby the Chancellor of the Exchequer was more sympathetic than other parts of the government as to the concerns of the financial industry. Third, the UK financial industry was not united on the issue of Brexit (see James and Quaglia 2017). Different parts of the financial industry would be impacted by Brexit in different ways, and the parts most likely to be badly affected were those that mobilised the most. The UK-based financial services most potentially affected were wholesale – not retail – because wholesale business is international and cross-border in nature. Thus, the financial services most affected by Brexit would be investment banking and clearing of euro denominated assets.

The four largest UK banks – HSBC, Royal Bank of Scotland (RBS), Barclays and Lloyds TSB – opposed Brexit. However, they were not very vocal in their opposition following the June 2016 referendum because they made limited use of the passport, their UK customer base included Brexit supporters and they did not want to antagonize the UK government (James and Quaglia 2017). Throughout 2017, UK banks announced 'contingency plans' to move staff and operations to the EU27, in the event that Brexit negotiations did not ensure full access to the Single Market. Lloyds TSB stated that it planned to convert its German branch in Berlin into a subsidiary, and so did Standard Charter with reference to its branch in Frankfurt. HSBC moved to enlarge its existing subsidiary in Paris and RBS announced similar plans with regard to its subsidiary in Dublin. Barclays announced its decision to establish a subsidiary in Dublin.

Big non-EU banks – first and foremost US banks – used the UK as a point of entry into the Single Market through UK-based subsidiaries that then branched out or conducted cross-border business in the EU. Approximately 90% of both European turnover and employees of the five large US investment banks (Goldman Sachs, JP Morgan, Citigroup, Morgan Stanley, Bank of America Merrill Lynch) were located in London (Schoenmaker 2016; Schoenmaker and Véron 2017). US banks were vocal opponents of Brexit, especially a hard Brexit, and were less restrained than UK banks in voicing their concerns publicly in the media and vis-à-vis the UK government, especially the Treasury. US banks preferred to lobby individually in the UK and announced plans to open offices in Frankfurt.[3] The degree to which these announced plans were part of a bank lobbying campaign to influence the UK government's negotiating position was unclear. To date, details on most bank staff transfers and office space expansion remained unclear. According to a number of sources, most banks were 'looking to minimize expense and disruption by relocating as little as possible in the first instance' (Oliver Wyman 2017; interview, Brussels, October 2017).

The other part of the UK financial sector that would be badly affected by Brexit, especially a hard Brexit, was *derivatives clearing*. Indeed, if clearing restrictions were imposed by the EU in the context of Brexit, the LCH.Clearnet Group would have a clear incentive to move its euro denominated clearing business from London to Paris or Frankfurt. This partly explains why the French and German governments were keen to restrict euro denominated clearing outside the EU, as elaborated in the following section. Hence, the London Stock Exchange (LSE), which was the main owner of LCH.Clearnet, repeatedly pointed out the need to avoid clearing restrictions in the context of Brexit (see, for example, Burton 2017).

The EU27 and Brexit: defending collective and national interests in finance

In the aftermath of the referendum, four interrelated dynamics in the EU27 are noteworthy. First, the European Commission, the Parliament and the EU27 member states, made clear that the four freedoms were indivisible and that there would not be a special deal for finance. The EU negotiating guidelines adopted by the European Council (2017: 3) stated that 'Preserving the integrity of the Single Market excludes participation based on a sector-by-sector approach … there can be no "cherry picking"'. Second, the Commission (2017) proposed the tightening up of the procedures for assessing equivalence for 'high impact third countries for which an equivalence decision may be used intensively by market operators' – notably the UK. The position of the member states on this tightening varied. While public official statements on equivalence are rare, French Ministry of Finance officials (interview, 16 June 2017) argued that equivalence rules had been excessively watered down in legislation – as in the Alternative Investment Fund Managers directive – and should be reinforced especially for 'high impact' third countries. The explicit French aim was to encourage UK firms to relocate operations to Paris. Certain other member states (interview, Ministry of Finance, Luxembourg, 29 June 2017; Asimakopoulos and Wright 2017), however, saw no need to reinforce equivalence rules.

Third, the European Central Bank (ECB), supported by the French and German central banks and governments, re-opened the issue of restricting the bulk of clearing of euro denominated assets to the EU – and, ideally, the euro area (*Financial Times*, 15 January 2017). In the aftermath of the Brexit referendum, French President François Hollande and the Governor of the Bank of France, François Villeroy de Galhau stated on separate occasions that the UK would not be able to retain its key role in clearing euro denominated assets (Skolimowski 2016). In early 2017, Andreas Dombret (2017) – a member of the Executive Board of the German Bundesbank – argued in favour of 'having the bulk of the clearing business inside the euro area'. In June 2017, the ECB, with the support of the Commission, proposed a change to its statutes that would give it and other euro area central banks a clear legal competence in the area of central clearing.

Fourth, the main EU27 financial centres and their public authorities began to mobilize to attract business, as detailed below. In May 2017, the European Securities and Markets Authority (ESMA 2017) issued guidance aimed at avoiding competition on regulatory and supervisory practices between member states, and a possible race to the bottom in the context of Brexit. ESMA subsequently developed sector-specific guidance concerning alternative investment funds, assets management and securities trading. Concerns about a potential race to the bottom and supervisory inconsistencies were also aired by the ECB and the Single Supervisory Board (SSB) (Lautenschläger 2017). In April 2017, the ECB published detailed guidance on several Brexit-related queries, stating that it was concerned with ensuring consistent supervision throughout the euro area and that the ECB would not give out licenses to 'empty shell companies' (ECB 2017a).

In France, the Governor of the Bank of France, Villeroy de Galhau, publicly proclaimed Brexit an opportunity for the euro area and, more specifically, for the Paris financial centre (Cuny 2017). In September 2016, the former Governor of the Bank of France, Christian Noyer was appointed as 'France's Brexit point man' with the explicit mission of attracting financial business to Paris. In the same month, the *Autorité de contrôle prudentiel et de résolution* (ACPR) – which monitors banks and insurers – and the *Autorité des marchés financiers* (AMF) – which safeguards investments and the stock market – issued a joint statement saying they were 'getting ready to welcome British-based institutions that wish to locate their business in France' (ACPR and AMF 2016). The joint statement specified that the licensing procedure would be simplified by using documents already available in English that have been submitted to the supervisory authorities in the home country, namely the UK.

The heads of French banks unanimously claimed that they were not preoccupied with the potential destabilization of Brexit and rather saw it as an opportunity for the French banking system, notably through the repatriation of certain operations undertaken by French banks in London (de Guigné 2017; interview with bank official, Paris, November 2017; Brassac 2017). Furthermore, the *Fédération bancaire française* (FBF) pointed out 'the need to create an ecosystem favourable to banks in order to attract them to Paris' (authors' translation) (Barbat Layani 2017). Despite the public expression of limited concern, French banks had the third largest exposure to the UK economy of any EU country's banks (after Germany and Spain).

In November 2016, Europlace produced a report 'Brexit: La Place de Paris en pôle position en Europe pour attirer les entreprises' (Europlace 2016). By using 12 criteria for the evaluation of financial centres, the report suggested that except for two criteria, Paris ranked higher than Frankfurt. However, in June 2017, a French Senate commission produced a report (de Montgolfier 2017) that argued that French reforms adopted to date were insufficient to make France (Paris) attractive to international financial firms and more needed to be done. With the election of a pro-finance Emmanuel Macron as President, the new French government announced a number of additional reforms to make Paris more attractive to international finance, including lower corporate taxes, reform to the wealth tax, the elimination of the highest bracket of payroll tax on employees, the cancellation of a planned extension of the financial transaction tax, the reduction of additional regulatory burdens, and the creation of a new commercial court for 'highly technical' legal disputes. The new prime minister, Edouard Philippe made the broader promise of keeping financial regulation to a minimum, insisting that France would move on from a past of 'over-regulation' (Bright 2017).

In Germany, national policy-makers were eager to attract potential financial business from London. German Finance Minister Wolfgang Schäuble discreetly supported the City of Frankfurt's efforts to attract thousands of bankers (O'Donnell 25 January 2017). In January 2017, German banking regulators met more than 20 foreign banks to spell out requirements to move operations to Frankfurt. The meeting was hosted by the financial supervisory authority, Bafin, which made clear that no 'letter-box' operations would be accepted and that banks would have to have significant risk management arrangements and senior executives based in Frankfurt (a point also made separately by the Bundesbank).

The President of the Association of German Private Banks (2016) optimistically stated that he was 'confident that Frankfurt [would] benefit from Britain leaving the EU'. The Association of German Private Banks (2017) also indicated that its member institutions would be relocating various operations from London to Germany over the next two years and that this was 'relatively straightforward from a regulatory and organizational point of view'. Yet, although the bulk of German banks were domestically oriented, the UK was their second-most important foreign market, immediately following the US. Moreover, German banks had significant exposure to the UK – about 22% of German GDP. UK banks' exposure to German counterparties represented 12% of UK GDP.

Similar to the actions of the French Europlace, the Frankfurt Finanzplatz commissioned the study 'Brexit – Let's go Frankfurt' (Helaba 2016). The study compared European financial centres, ranking Frankfurt in second place behind London. Like Paris, Frankfurt was keen to attract clearing derivatives business, as stated by the head of Finanzplatz Deutschland, Hubertus Väth (Colson 2017). In October 2017, Deutsche Börse moved to attract the clearing of euro denominated derivatives contracts from London by changing its clearing rules.

An overall assessment: 'battle' amongst member states or transnational coalitions?

The explanation based on transnational financial networks and the new interdependence fits well with the arguments used by the Bank of England, the UK government, and part of the UK based financial industry (e.g., the LSE). For example, the Governor of the Bank of England, Mark Carney (2017a, 2017b) argued that there was a mutual interest in a special deal for finance given that London was the 'investment banker' for the EU. Carney (2017a, 2017b) also warned against the fragmentation of global markets by jurisdiction or currency on the grounds that this would reduce the benefits of central clearing. The chairman of the LSE (Rolet 2016) pointed out that the disaggregation of the euro component of the LCH interest rate swap engine Swap Clear would cost the financial services industry $77 billion of additional margins (a similar) point was made in a policy paper by the Intercontinental Exchange (ICE 2016).

However, the ECB (2017b) and some EU27 national central banks and regulatory agencies explicitly downplayed and/or challenged concerns about the implications of Brexit for financial stability or credit provision in the EU27. For example, in November 2016, Bundesbank Executive Board member, Andreas Dombret (2016) pointed out that

> it is often argued that if Brexit hampered the banking sector, it might impair the financing of the European economy. I don't share those fears. Brexit and its possible repercussions for the City of London are unlikely to be an issue for financial stability or the financing of the EU's real economy.

French authorities – both in the public sector and banking sector – were generally unwilling to raise the prospect of EU-wide financial instability caused by Brexit (interview, banking association official, Paris, November 2017), despite the high level of financial integration between the French and UK economies – albeit lower than between Germany and the UK.

The French government and ministry of finance also took a hard line on the need for a tough EU negotiation position with the UK and the sanctity of the Single Market. In contrast, the German Ministry of Finance prepared a study (internal paper), stressing that Germany had considerable interest in an 'integrated financial market' with the UK – given the high level of financial integration between the UK and German economies – but this was to be subject to the latter respecting EU regulatory conditions (Boerse-online.de, 27 March 2017).

As for private actors, one of the main European financial lobbying groups – the Association for Financial Markets in Europe (AFME) – campaigned in coordination with City lobbying groups (including the British Bankers' Association (BBA)) in favour of a long transition period for finance (AFME 2017). The AFME argued that Brexit created particular uncertainty for cross-border wholesale banking. The other main European financial lobby group, the European Bankers' Federation (EBF) – which represents 32 national banking associations – adopted a more neutral position but nonetheless encouraged both the EU27 member states and the UK to provide clarity and certainty on

Brexit and financial matters as soon as possible to diminish the risk of financial instability (interview with a major EU27 national banking association official, Brussels, 15 November 2017).

There is no publicly available evidence to date that any EU27 national financial associations or major financial companies sought to form a transnational coalition with financial sector actors across the Channel to put pressure on EU and member state authorities to reach a special deal on finance. A number of interviewees explicitly noted the lack of a transnational coalition and the tendency of EU-headquartered banks and associations to be sensitive – albeit reluctantly – to different national government positions.

> The problem in these EU associations has been that each industry national segment looks closely at the political position of their home country and tends to align with it. So those who are headquartered in a country that sees Brexit as an opportunity to attract business away from London tend to disengage from any effort to find common solutions (interview with UK bank official, Brussels, 17 November 2017).

> Their silence [on the costs of Brexit to EU27 banks] is surprising to some extent. But it is a deeply uncomfortable territory for companies. Companies are usually cautious with politics, and Brexit is the most political thing happening in a long time, so I can understand their silence. They doubt whether they can have any influence on it and they wonder how they might be thanked for it afterwards (interview with UK bank official, Brussels, 17 November 2017).

A French bank official (interview, Paris, 29 November 2017, authors' translation) remarked that:

> our only real concern is to not rise above our station, not to interfere with the political debate, which is very tense because potential political costs are very high. We are merely merchants. Hence we focus on technical points, we do not comment on (dis)agreements between governments.

An official of a major EU27 banking association (interview, Brussels, 15 November 2017) reiterated that:

> A deal on finance that would leave us as close as possible to the previous situation would be the preference of [national association] members, but we have to be aware that this is impossible due to political forces, and prepare for no deal.

Officials from several major EU financial associations also noted their frustration with the prioritization of national politics over a deal that would minimize disruption. Some officials specifically targeted French companies:

> the French government and the broader French establishment have taken a very strong stance on Brexit. ... It feels like the political position of the French banking sector is defined in the Elysée [the French president's office] and passed on to the banks. When we talk to French banks individually, they seem to worry about the consequences of Brexit, but collectively there is not

a word of that (interview, EU financial association officials, Brussels, 21 November 2017).

A number of EU27 national associations met with the UK-based International Regulatory Strategy Group (IRSG) and the UK bank lobby group UK Finance to discuss proposals for a 'mutual access' agreement (see *Financial Times*, 3 July 2017). However, the widespread view of these national associations was that certain EU27 governments would not 'let this fly' and these transnational efforts fizzled out (interview with a major EU27 national banking association official, 15 November 2017). This absence of a transnational coalition and the alignment with national government positions remains surprising given widespread support in EU27-headquartered banks and national banking associations for a special carve out on finance and concerns regarding the significant predicted costs of having to capitalize their UK branches which, without a special deal on finance, would potentially have to be transformed into subsidiaries. However, in December 2017, the UK Prudential Regulation Authority provided reassurances concerning the treatment of branches of European banks in the UK after Brexit (Jack 2017), although the implications (and the costs for European banks in the future) remained to be seen.

US-headquartered financial institutions, acting alone or in coordination with US public authorities, encouraged a special deal on finance. US banks were concerned about the cost of establishing or expanding subsidiaries in the EU27 because of the need to meet EU and national capital requirements. US bank efforts were largely channelled through the AFME, whose chairman was Michael Cole-Fontayne, head of Europe at Bank of New York Mellon. The AFME appears to have been the most important group leading transnational efforts to push for a special deal for finance (Martin 2017; Williams-Grut 2017).

There was a 'battle' between the main financial centres in the EU27 in order to lure business from London, building on national competitive advantages mainly resulting from the configuration of national financial systems. The main continental financial centres, first and foremost Paris and Frankfurt, competed directly with each other in order to attract business from London. For example, at an event in London in October 2016, representatives of business lobbies from both Paris (Europlace) and Frankfurt (Finanzplatz Deutschland) pitched hard to the business community that their cities should be the preferred destination for relocation (*Business Insider*, 19 October 2016). Rivalries among EU27 financial centres and among their member state government backers also surfaced in the case of euro clearing, where German, French and Italian policy-makers argued that the ECB should only be given authority over non-EU clearing houses engaged in significant levels of euro clearing, but not those in the EU (Canepa and Koranyi 2017). Overall, EU institutions adopted official neutrality on the attractiveness of different EU27 financial centres.

It is puzzling that in the case of Brexit there was a battle for financial services amongst the member states, while at the same time an EU-wide transnational coalition did not materialize. This is unlike what happened, for example, in the re-launch of the completion of the Single Market in finance prior to the international financial crisis. Two factors account for this battle and absence of transnational coalition: the political salience of Brexit and the competing financial interests that Brexit generated. First, Brexit was an issue of high 'salience' for politicians and public opinion in the UK and EU, whereas the financial industry traditionally yields more influence on matters of 'quiet politics' (Culpepper 2011). The influence of powerful economic interests is high when decisions are largely insulated from political pressures (Culpepper 2011; Pagliari 2013), but it declines when decisions face greater public scrutiny. In this context, politicians are more likely to respond to voters' concerns than to financial industry structural and instrumental power. The high political salience of Brexit reduced the willingness of politicians to listen to business concerns and therefore limited the incentives and ability of the financial industry on both sides of the Channel to lobby for a special deal in finance.

The UK government was less sympathetic to the Brexit-related concerns raised by the financial industry than it was on most national and EU regulatory issues. James and Quaglia (2017) report that City lobbyists found it difficult to access the Prime Minister's office and that business groups would be 'frozen out' if they were too negative on Brexit. In the EU, national political authorities made clear that there would be no cherry picking of the Single Market (especially for finance) and that they expected their national business communities to support the positions taken by their respective national governments. For example, at the beginning of the Brexit negotiations in June 2017, Chancellor Merkel warned the German business community to 'hold firm' and 'don't let anyone drive a wedge between us' (Delfs 2017).

Second, the financial industry in the UK and EU27 had (partly) competing interests. The main financial centres in the EU27 had an interest in attracting business from the UK, whereas the UK-based financial industry had the opposite interest. Moreover, when trade associations and individual UK and US banks sought to liaise with their counterparts in the EU, they were perceived as making the case for a special deal in finance on behalf of the UK government (James and Quaglia 2017). The financial industry and regulators on both sides of the Channel also had an interest in avoiding major disruptions in cross-border financial flows, the functioning of the Single Market in finance and financial stability. Yet, politics appears to have trumped economics in the context of Brexit.

The two theoretical frameworks applied in this paper are focused in large part upon dynamics created by financial interests. However, one should be aware of the explanatory limits of these two frameworks. Indeed, certain aspects of the negotiations concerning Brexit and finance – for example, the decision of the UK government to downplay the calls of parts of the City of London for a soft Brexit and the concerns raised by the ECB against continuing to rely on the City as the main centre for the clearing of euro denominated swaps – cannot be adequately explained by these two theoretical frameworks.[4] Nonetheless, a neo-mercantilist 'battle' amongst member states approach remains the most convincing explanation for the positioning of the German and French governments and their financial centres.

Conclusion

In this paper, we have used two main theoretical approaches derived from the existing literature on the political-economy of European financial integration to shed light on the implications of Brexit for finance and the dynamics that have been unleashed. Our findings suggest that some 'transnational alliances' on the subject of finance and Brexit were formed as the result of financial interdependence. Yet, these alliances were limited in scope and failed to involve or mobilize significantly EU private and public sector actors. In the private sector, the AFME – one of the main EU-level lobbying groups – and several UK-based financial associations argued for a long transition period for finance following the conclusion of Brexit negotiations and, ideally, a special deal on finance. In the public sector, a number of German (and other EU27) officials noted their awareness of the importance of the City of London in European finance and reiterated the arguments presented by both UK public authorities and a range of UK-based financial companies and their representative associations (Asimakopoulos and Wright 2017). The main caveat to be noted with regard to this conclusion about the lobbying efforts and demands of international finance, is that it remained possible that transnational coalitions involving EU partners could gain momentum as Brexit negotiations progressed.

There is far greater evidence of a neo-mercantilist 'battle' amongst member states, with individual national governments promoting their financial centres and competing to attract financial operations from the UK. Frankfurt was touted as the main destination for banks. French efforts to improve the attractiveness of Paris had limited success to the time of writing (April 2018), although the 2017 election of Emmanuel Macron boded well for further reform. In this context, the EU authorities, namely the Commission and the ECB, were keen to preserve the integrity of the Single Market and its four freedoms. They sought to prevent a regulatory 'race to the bottom' in finance – with financial centres and national authorities attempting to undercut each other – thus undermining longstanding efforts to construct a level playing field across the EU.

Notes

1. We wish to thank an anonymous reviewer for this point.
2. Equivalence rules stipulate that unless third country rules are equivalent to EU rules, foreign firms providing services in the EU or doing business with EU counterparts would be subject to EU regulation in addition to their home country regulation. Without equivalence, foreign firms failing to respect EU regulations would be blocked from accessing the Single Market.
3. According to Frankfurt Main Finance – the main financial sector promotion body of the City of Frankfurt – quoted in the *Handelsblatt*, 26 April 2017.
4. We wish to thank an anonymous reviewer for this point.

Acknowledgements

The authors would like to thank Sébastien Commain – currently a doctoral student at the University of Luxembourg and research assistant to Professor Howarth – for his help conducting a number of interviews with financial company and association representatives in Brussels and Paris. This paper was partly written while Lucia Quaglia was a research fellow at the Scuola Normale Superiore, Florence.

Disclosure statement

No potential conflict of interest was reported by the authors.

References

ACPR and AMF (2016) 'L'ACPR et l'AMF simplifient et accélèrent les procédures d'agrément dans le contexte du BREXIT', Communication de presse, 28 Septembre, available at https://acpr.banque-france.fr/fileadmin/user_upload/acp/Communication/Communiques%20de%20presse/20160928-CP-ACPR-AMF-agreme nts-Brexit.pdf.

Armstrong, K. (2018) 'Regulatory alignment and divergence after Brexit', *Journal of European Public Policy*, doi:10.1080/13501763.2018.1467956.

Association for Financial Markets in Europe (AMFE) (2017) 'Implementing Brexit: practical challenges for wholesale banking in adapting to the new environment', April, available at https://www.afme.eu/globalassets/downloads/publications/afme-implementing-brexit-2017.pdf.

Association of German Private Banks (2016) *Press Statement*, available at https://bankenverband.de/newsroom/presse-infos/president-association-german-banks-regrets-decision-brexit/.

Association of German Private Banks (2017), *Press Statement*, available at https://bankenverband.de/newsroom/presse-infos/impact-brexit-german-banks-will-be-limited/.

Asimakopoulos, P. and Wright, W. (2017) 'What the rest of the EU thinks about Brexit and the City of London', *New Financial*, available at 2017.04-What-the-rest-of-the-EU-thinks-about-Brexit-New-Financial-FINAL1.pdf.

Barbat Layani, M.A. (2017) *Press Statement*, available at http://www.fbf.fr/fr/espace-presse/interventions-de-la-fbf/marie-anne-barbat-layani-au-iveme-forum-du-grand-paris---il-faut-creer-un-ecosysteme-favorable-aux-banques-pour-les-attirer-a-paris.

Bank of England (2015) 'Mapping the UK financial system', *Bank of England Quarterly Bulletin*, Q2, London.

Batsaikhan, U., Kalcik, R. and Schoenmaker, D. (2017) 'Brexit and the European financial system: mapping markets, players and jobs', Bruegel Institute, Policy contribution, Issue 4, available at http://bruegel.org/wp-content/uploads/2017/02/PC-04-2017-finance-090217-final.pdf.

Brassac, P. (2017) 'Interview de Philippe Brassac, Président de la FBF, Directeur général de Crédit Agricole SA, pour Revue Banque – "Le système bancaire français est un ilot de stabilité dans un monde d'incertitudes", FBF website, 9 January, available at http://www.fbf.fr/fr/espace-presse/interventions-de-la-fbf/interview-de-philippe-brassac,-president-de-la-fbf,-directeur-general-de-credit-agricole-sa,-pour-revue-banque---le-systeme-bancaire-francais-est-un-ilot-de-stabilite-dans-un-monde-d'incertitudes.

Bright, R. (2017) 'Paris rolls out 'red-white-and-blue carpet' for banks', *Financial Times*, 7 July.

Bulmer, S. and Quaglia, L. (2018) 'Introduction', Journal of European Public Policy, doi:10.1080/13501763.2018.1467957.

Burton, L. (2017) 'LSE fires back at EU plot to seize euro-clearing', *The Telegraph*, 2 May.

Canepa, F. and Koranyi, B. (2017) 'Exclusive: ECB plan to take euro clearing from London stalled by infighting – sources', 22 May, Reuters, available at http://www.reuters.com/article/us-britain-eu-clearing-ecb-idUSKBN18I1B2.

Carney, M. (2017a) 'Oral evidence', Treasury Committee, House of Commons 11 January.

Carney, M. (2017b) 'A Fine Balance, speech at Mansion House', Bank of England, 20 June, London.

The CityUK (2016a) *The Impact of the UKs Exit from the EU on the UK Based Financial Services Sector*, October, available at https://www.thecityuk.com/assets/2016/Reports-PDF/The-impact-of-the-UKs-exit-from-the-EU-on-the-UK-based-financial-services-sector.pdf.

The CityUK (2016b), *Brexit and the industry*, September, available at https://www.thecityuk.com/research/brexit-and-the-industry/.

Colson, T. (2017) 'Frankfurt is 'confident in the arguments' for poaching Britain's €930 billion euro clearing industry after Brexit', Business Insider UK, 7 July, available at http://uk.businessinsider.com/brexit-relocation-financial-services-frankfurt-main-2017-7.

Commission (2017), 'Commission staff working document EU equivalence decisions in financial services policy: an assessment', Brussels, 27 February.

Culpepper, P. D. (2011) *Quiet Politics and Business Power: Corporate Control in Europe and Japan*, Cambridge: Cambridge University Press.

Cuny, D. (2017) 'Brexit Paris a toutes ses chances selon Villeroy de Galhau', *La Tribune*, 29 May.

de Guigné, A. (2017) 'Brexit: Paris veut améliorer sa copie pour attirer plus d'entreprises', *Le Figaro*, 24 July.

Delfs, A. (2017) 'Merkel tells German industry to hold firm as Brexit talks begin', *Bloomberg*, 20 June.

Dombret, A. (2016) 'What does Brexit mean for European banks', Keynote Speech at a Conference of the Association of German Banks Center for Financial Studies, Goethe University Frankfurt, 13 July, available at https://www.bundesbank.de/Redaktion/EN/Reden/2016/2016_07_13_dombret.html.

Dombret, A. (2017) 'Andreas Dombret: Uncertain times – Brexit and its impact on the financial sector', Remarks to Boston Consulting Group, Frankfurt am Main, 7 February, available at http://www.bis.org/review/r170208a.pdf.

European Central Bank (ECB) (2017a) 'Relocating to the euro area', available at https://www.bankingsupervision.europa.eu/banking/relocating/html/index.en.html.

European Central Bank (ECB) (2017b) *Financial Stability Review*, May, available at https://www.ecb.europa.eu/pub/pdf/other/ecb.financialstabilityreview201705.en.pdf?ce0cddcde1256fb5f6653e8aedf2ebd7.

European Council (2017) 'Special meeting of the European Council (Art. 50) (29 April 2017) – Guidelines', Brussels, 29 April, EUCO XT 20004/17, BXT 10, CO EUR 5, CONCL 2, available at 29-euco-art50-guidelines.en.pdf.

European Securities Markets Authority (ESMA) (2017) *Principles on the Supervisory Approach on Relocations from the UK*, available at https://www.esma.europa.eu/press-news/esma-news/esma-issues-principles-supervisory-approach-relocations-uk.

Europlace (2016) 'The Paris marketplace in pole position to attract companies', Press Conference slides, 29 November, available at http://www.paris-europlace.com/sites/default/files/public/the_paris_marketplace_in_pole_position_-_28112016_en.pdf.

Farrell, H. and Newman A. (2015) 'The new politics of interdependence: cross-national layering in trans-atlantic regulatory disputes', *Comparative Political Studies* 48(4): 497–526.

Farrell, H. and Newman, A. (2016) 'The new interdependence approach: theoretical development and empirical demonstration', *Review of International Political Economy* 23(5): 713–36.

Farrell, H. and Newman, A. (2017) 'Brexit, voice and loyalty: rethinking electoral politics in an age of interdependence', *Review of International Political Economy* 24 (2): 232–47.

Fioretos, O. (2010) 'Capitalist diversity and the international regulation of hedge funds', *Review of International Political Economy* 17(3): 696–723.

Ford, J. (2017) 'An equivalence deal on Brexit may be the best the City can get', *Financial Times*, 10 April.

Graz, C. and Noelke, A. (eds) (2008) *Transnational Private Governance and its Limits*, London: Routledge.

Helaba (2016) 'Brexit — Let's Go Frankfurt', *Financial Centre Focus*, 3 November, available at https://www.helaba.com/blob/com/408348/c00d2e172a25dd521fab5df9e34c795c/financial-centre-focus--brexit---let-s-go-frankfurt-data.pdf.

Howarth, D. (2013) 'France and the international financial crisis: the legacy of state-led finance', *Governance: An International Journal of Policy, Administration, and Institutions* 26(3): 369–95.

Howarth, D. and Quaglia, L. (2013) 'Banking on stability: the political economy of new capital requirements in the European Union', *Journal of European Integration* 35(3): 333–46.

ICE (2016) 'Access to global markets', Working Paper, available at https://www.theice. com/publicdocs/ICE_Working_Paper_Access_Global_Markets.pdf.

Jack, S. (2017) 'Brexit: UK plans to soften impact on European banks', *BBC*, 20 December.

James, S. and Quaglia, L. (2017) 'Brexit and the limits of financial power in the UK', Working Paper, University of Oxford, available at https://www.geg.ox.ac.uk/brexit-and-limits-financial-power-uk.

Krotz, U. and Schild, J. (2018) 'Back to the future? Brexit and Franco-German bilateralism in Europe's Union', *Journal of European Public Policy*, doi:10.1080/13501763.2018. 1467951.

Lautenschläger, S. (2017) 'Some supervisory expectations for banks relocating to the euro area', Technical workshop for banks considering relocation in the context of Brexit, Frankfurt am Main, 4 May, available at https://www.bankingsupervision. europa.eu/press/speeches/date/2017/html/ssm.sp170504.en.html (accessed 25 June 2017).

Lütz, S. (1998) 'The revival of the nation-state? Stock exchange regulation in an era of globalized financial markets', *Journal of European Public Policy* 5(1): 153–68.

Macartney, H. (2010) *Variegated Neoliberalism: EU Varieties of Capitalism and International Political Economy*, London: Routledge.

Martin, B. (2017) 'London and Brussels urged to agree Brexit transition deal to protect banks', *The Telegraph*, 5 April.

de Montgolfier, A. (2017) 'Places financières : quelle stratégie française face au *Brexit* ?', Rapport d'information 574 (Report presented to the French Senate), 7 June 2017, available at https://www.senat.fr/notice-rapport/2016/r16-574-notice.html.

Mügge, D. (2010) *Widen the Market, Narrow the Competition: Banker Interests and the Making of a European Capital Market*, Colchester: ECPR.

Newman, A. and Posner E. (2016) 'Transnational feedback, soft law, and preferences in global financial regulation', *Review of International Political Economy* 23(1): 123–52.

O'Donnell, (2017) 'Germany calls bankers to Frankfurt for Brexit move talks', *Reuters*, 25 January.

Pagliari, S. (2013) 'Public salience and international financial Regulation', *Thesis presented to the* University of Waterloo.

Posner, E. (2009) *The Origins of Europe's New Stock Markets*, Cambrdige, MA: Harvard University Press.

Quaglia, L. (2010) *Governing Financial Services in the European Union: Banking, Securities and Post-Trading*, London: Routledge.

Rolet, X. (2016) 'Oral Evidence, Brexit: financial services', 9th Report of Session 2016-17, European Union Committee, House of Lords, December.

Schoenmaker, D. (2016) 'Lost passports: a guide to the Brexit fallout for the City of London', Bruegel Institute, Blog, 30 June, available at http://bruegel.org/2016/06/lost-passports-a-guide-to-the-brexit-fallout-for-the-city-of-london/.

Schoenmaker, D., and Véron, N. (2017) 'Making the best of Brexit', February, available at http://bruegel.org/wp-content/uploads/2017/02/Bruegel_Policy_Brief-2017_01-060217.pdf.

Skolimowski, P. (2016) 'Draghi says clearing oversight after Brexit is "crucial" for ECB', *Bloomberg*, 29 June.

Story, J., and Walter, I. (1997) *Political Economy of Financial Integration in Europe: The Battle of the System*, Manchester: Manchester University Press.

Tsingou, E. (2008). 'Transnational private governance and the Basel process: banking regulation, private interests and Basel II', in J.C. Graz and A. Nölke (eds), *Transnational Private Governance and its Limits*. London: Routledge, 58–68.

UK government (2017) 'The United Kingdom's exit from, and new partnership with, the European Union white paper', 2 February, available at https://www.gov.uk/government/publications/the-united-kingdoms-exit-from-and-new-partnership-with-the-european-union-white-paper.

Van Apeldoorn, B. (2002) *Transnational Capitalism and the Struggle Over European Integration*, London: Routledge.

Williams-Grut, O. (2017) 'Hard Brexit: execs are lobbying Brussels to stop it', *Business Insider*, 3 July.

Wyman, O. (2017) 'One year on from the Brexit vote: a briefing for wholesale banks', available at http://www.oliverwyman.com/content/dam/oliver-wyman/v2/publications/2017/aug/OW-Wholesale-Banking-Brexit-Briefing.pdf.

Brexit and the perils of 'Europeanised' migration

James Dennison ⓘ and Andrew Geddes

ABSTRACT
Moving beyond short-term public opinion accounts for Brexit this article considers how Britain's historic policy and political dynamics on migration led to the outcome of the EU referendum and how the latter is likely to transform current immigration policies. To do so, we explore historic and theoretical tensions in UK migration policy and politics over the last six decades. We show how these unresolved tensions allowed Eurosceptics to harness negative attitudes to the increasingly salient issue of immigration. We argue that a sufficient proportion of the UK's elite and electorate proved unable and unwilling to subordinate its desire for entirely domestic 'control' over immigration to the EU's right-based regime, let alone see fellow EU citizens in the UK as anything other than immigrants, ultimately giving Leave victory. The referendum process and outcome exposed the debate about free movement and migration to much wider public scrutiny and so raised more profound questions about the future of the British economy and the political model necessary to sustain it. We argue that, with the Brexit negotiations under constant public scrutiny a new, largely immovable parameter was set by the EU referendum result for the medium term that seems likely to lead to a decline in 'Europeanised' migration policy in the UK.

Introduction

Never was the politics of immigration in the UK quite so 'Europeanised' as the moment at which the country chose to leave the European Union (EU). Immigration politics had become Europeanised in terms of the magnitude of flows of EU citizens to the UK, the attendant economic reliance on EU citizens in key economic sectors and the way that British politics became subject to populist mobilisations over EU free movement and immigration to which it was previously seen as resistant, perhaps even immune. Underpinning this economic and migratory Europeanisation were the EU's citizens' rights and four freedoms legal framework, which together guaranteed rights to move to the UK for all EEA (European Economic Area) nationals and guaranteed socio-economic rights, most notably to work and to receive some social assistance.

49

Crucially, however, Europeanisation did not extend to a transformation of popular identities in the UK, which remained nationally-oriented and, by EU standards, anomalously non-European. The result of this clash between the lack of British European identity and the intensification of Europeanisation of immigration – both legally and demographically – was a triggering of latent British Euroscepticism, which was already pronounced by the twenty-first century. This Euroscepticism, initially a constitutional and monetary issue, became fused with the highly salient matter of immigration and identity concerns.

We consider these, at first glance, distinct observations as crucial for answering two questions about Brexit. First, how did 'immigration' – both in terms of policy and public opinion – lead to Brexit? And, second, what do these observations tell us about the likely parameters for a post-Brexit migration regime? Our analysis goes beyond short-termist public opinion accounts for Brexit and the role of 'EU immigration' therein by considering the more fundamental tensions and structures of migration politics and policy in the UK over the last six decades, offering a theoretical and historical explanation.

We locate these questions within a broader tension between 'functionalist' and 'postfunctionalist' perspectives on European integration (Hooghe and Marks 2009). Theories of European integration have traditionally been centred on whether the impetus to European integration derived from national governments or from supranational actors such as the European Commission, while the analytical focus remained on elite bargaining. Since the creation by the Maastricht Treaty of the European Union and its movement into areas of high politics (Economic and Monetary Union, Justice and Home Affairs), popular opposition has become more evident, marking a move from an elite-enabling 'permissive consensus' to a 'constraining dissensus'. More profoundly, these constraints signified a greater role for 'postfunctional' identity-based concerns that were particularly evident in debate about migration and free movement in the UK. The result was that 'a brake on European integration has been imposed not because people have changed their minds, but because, on a range of vital issues, legitimate decision making has shifted from an insulated elite to mass politics' (Hooghe and Marks 2009: 13). Consistent with this postfunctional account, our account of migration governance in the context of Brexit has three components: first, the politicisation of immigration marked by increased issue salience; second an increasingly decisive role for general public preferences rather than the views of more concentrated interests such as the business lobby; and, third, identity concerns that became 'critical in shaping contestation on Europe' (Hooghe and Marks 2009: 1).

The article is organised into four sections. The first section develops an account of UK immigration policy that specifies in more detail the tension between a functional approach to migration policy and an identity-based post-functional dynamic. The second section accounts for the activation of latent, relatively strong Euroscepticism in Britain by unexpectedly high levels of movement to the UK by EU citizens, culminating in Cameron's pledge of a renegotiation and referendum. The third considers the role of immigration and free movement in the EU referendum campaign and vote. Finally, in the fourth section, we apply our conceptual approach and the identification of a tension between functional and post-functional dynamics to consider the parameters of the UK's post-Brexit migration regime.

Europeanised migration in the UK

From 2004 onwards, 'immigration' to the UK became increasingly 'Europeanised'. The term Europeanisation is most often used to refer to the degree to which a state's policies, politics or laws are harmonised with those of the EU, the extent to which national actors shape or are shaped by the EU, or, less frequently, the degree of micro-level Europeanised behaviour among citizens (Bulmer and Radaelli 2004; Favell *et al*. 2011). We here refer to three distinct types of Europeanisation. First, there has been an extensive Europeanisation of flows of people coming to live and work in the UK. Between 1993 and 2017, the EU-born population in the UK increased from just over 1 million to 3.7 million. After a decade of near continuous increase, in early 2014, the number of EU nationals moving to the UK outnumbered the number of non-EU nationals doing so for the first time. Second, the extent to which individuals identify as European, an increasingly common phenomenon in most EU member states (see Eurobarometer, 1992–2016), has remained stubbornly low in the UK (contra the logic of Deutsch *et al*. 1957; Kuhn 2011). Finally, there are significant limits to the UK government's engagement with the EU's free movement, migration and asylum policy framework through non-participation in Schengen passport-free travel and various opt-outs.

The broad-brush term 'immigration' has only limited analytical utility because it disguises a much more complex reality of varying motives for migration (to work, to study, to join with family members or to seek refuge being four key types), socio-demographic characteristics of migrants, durations of stay and also categorical ambiguities and misspecifications. A crucial distinction needs to be made from the outset. Under European Union law, movement of persons between member states is rights-based. Within the EU, citizens are guaranteed the right to move freely within the EU's internal borders by the Treaty on the Functioning of the European Union and the European Parliament and Council Directive 2004/38/EC of 29 April 2004, known as the Citizens' Rights Directive. This directive consolidated a number of older regulations and directives dating back to the 1960s. Beyond movement, EU citizens are also guaranteed a range of social and economic rights, including the right to work in any member state, which from the 1960s onwards has been broadened successively to include all economic activity as well as study and retirement. Although the right to unconditional residence is limited to three months if no treaty right related to economic activity is exercised, in practice citizens can generally move freely for an unlimited period given the broad remit of economic activity.

In contrast, immigration policy for non-EU nationals to the UK, and elsewhere in the wider EEA, is permission-based (Carmel *et al.* 2011). As such, the British government retains and uses the right to discriminate between would-be immigrants on grounds of nationality, skill-level and family reunification status, amongst other criteria. Previous waves of immigration to the UK had also been enabled by free movement frameworks, which subsequent UK governments replaced with a permission-based framework. Following the Second World War until 1962 most people coming to the UK arrived either from the Republic of Ireland under the provisions of a free movement framework (the 'Common Travel Area') or from Britain's colonies and ex-colonies as subjects of the Crown with a right to move to the UK under the terms of the 1948 British Nationality Act. Between 1962 and 1981, legislation on immigration and citizenship was introduced that enabled a retreat from a rights-based and expansive view of 'imperial citizenship'.

The term 'EU immigration', despite its ubiquity in the UK, is problematic because, pre-Brexit, EU citizens moved in the context of a rights-based treaty framework and therefore were not 'immigrants' in any legal sense. Some argue that it has been a triumph for the arguments of the populist right UK Independence Party (UKIP) that the term 'EU immigrant' managed so decisively to enter public debate and also academic interpretations of Brexit (Favell and Barbulescu 2018), although, as we argue, UKIP's ability to do this was partly endogenous to Britain's long-standing weak sense of pan-European identity.

The term 'immigration' is also analytically limited in terms of political attitudes. Individuals tend to have multidimensional attitudes to immigration (Sobolewska *et al.* 2016), both in terms of support for immigration of different groups – the highly educated, highly skilled, native language speaking and those from a similar cultural background being most favoured – and in terms of the various perceived effects of immigration – with immigration *in toto* perceived to have negative effects on some areas (e.g., crime) while simultaneously having positive effects on others (e.g., the economy) (European Social Survey Round 8 2016). Such complexities do not easily fit with a referendum campaign that boiled complex questions about migration and free movement into a binary choice. Moreover, whereas 'immigration' by EU nationals receives greater support than immigration by non-EU nationals in most western European countries, Britons on average show a smaller distinction between the two categories (Eurobarometer 86.1 2016). Finally, although immigration and European integration have both been historically controversial issues in Britain, they were not until the 2000s conjoined as political concerns. Until the early 2000s, free movement of people was a marginal phenomenon of relatively small numbers of people while academic enquiries into immigration were often linked to ideas of race and race relations (Geddes and Scholten 2016).

We suggest that there are important points of connection between analytical approaches of immigration and of European integration, and attitudes to each among the UK electorate, that allow us to consider how the referendum crystallised already existing social and political tensions and dynamics that strongly affected the outcome and are likely to shape the exit negotiations. To elucidate these connections requires consideration of the underlying dynamics of migration policy-making and, more particularly, the constellations of interests and action that can drive or determine policy. We contrast more focused, elite-driven and 'functional' forms of policy making that can potentially lead to more expansive outcomes for labour migration, on the one hand, with forms of immigration politics subject to wider public debate and scrutiny that can push towards a more restrictive approach, on the other. We argue that a form of elite-driven policy-making linked to labour market needs and business interests that developed in the early 2000s – a historic anomaly – became increasingly challenged, reaching its peak in the conduct and result of the 2016 referendum.

UK immigration policy has traditionally been predicated on a balance between numbers and integration that was summed up by then Home Office minister Roy Hattersley in 1966. As he put it: 'integration without control is impossible, but control without integration is indefensible' (cited in Favell 1998: 104). The history of British immigration policy meant that the Leave campaign slogan of 'take back control' resonated because this had long been the aim of government policy. The same could be said of the infamous and misleading 'breaking point' poster unveiled by Nigel Farage one week before the referendum, which showed a queue of refugees crossing the border from Croatia to Slovenia in summer 2015. The campaign exposed the unwillingness of sections of the electorate to subordinate the desire for immigration control, as part of a perceived balance between numbers and integration, to the EU's free movement framework, which necessarily undermines that balance as the cornerstone of the previous British political consensus on immigration.

The referendum campaign and outcome also suggested that the dynamics of migration policy were shifting in a postfunctional 'who are we' direction. This in itself is not necessarily new because concerns about control have tended to supersede arguments for openness. For a brief period in the early 2000s, there was openness to labour migration driven by economic arguments with powerful and well-organised business groups prepared to make the case for an expansive approach and with a receptive government. Writing about the period from the 1950s until the 1980s, Freeman noted that British 'governments have steadfastly ignored the economic consequences of immigration even when (as if often the case) these would almost certainly have been positive' (Freeman 1995: 298). The pursuit of control as a key policy objective meant that the British government refused to participate in the Schengen agreement after 1984 because the UK would not give up passport controls. Meanwhile the UK also opted out of key components of the EU migration and asylum acquis.

Ford *et al.* (2015) distinguish between three periods when assessing the relationship between migration and public opinion. The first from 1982 to 1997 was characterised by tight controls on immigration and very low levels of public concern. By contrast, between 1997 and 2004, Ford *et al* identify a 'selective liberalisation' with increased inflows of labour migrants and an increased demand for restriction. The decision by the Blair government to allow immediate access in 2004 to the UK labour market for the 10 accession states, including eight central and eastern European countries was truly momentous. Of western European member states, only Ireland and Sweden made a similar choice. This exposed a functional approach, driven above all by labour market concerns and the maintenance of an extremely pro-business image for the Labour Party, which, also ideologically, chimed with New Labour modernisation of the UK economy and society. EU free movement was linked to a liberal, deregulated UK labour market to which flexible, migrant labour became crucial (Anderson and Ruhs 2010).

After 2004, Ford *et al* show that levels of public concern rose with high levels of immigration, including EU free movement, creating a tension between a government that is 'responsive' to public attitudes and one that is 'responsible' given the economic contributions of EU citizens and demands in key economic sectors for labour from other EU member states. This 'responsive-responsible' dichotomy had already been identified by Mair (2014), who argued that increasingly technocratic, 'responsible' decision making, associated in part with European integration, had led to a 'hollowing out' of democratic politics. Over the ten years following the 2004 enlargement, this 'hollowed out' democratic politics would find itself surpassed by calls for a *direct* referendum on EU membership.

David Cameron, as leader of the Conservatives, was therefore walking a thin line when he sought to both modernise the Conservative Party and reduce net migration to the tens of thousands. The invention of a 'net migration target' was a short-term tactic masquerading as long-term strategy. This was a politically dangerous objective, though successful at the 2010 and 2015 general elections, because levels of net migration had been consistently running at more than 200,000 each year since 2004 and because his government lacked the legal power to implement such a change. During the referendum campaign itself, the Office for National Statistics (ONS) estimated that net migration to the UK – including those from EU countries – hit a record level of 332,000. UKIP and, later, the pro-Leave campaigns, were swift to claim that leaving the EU was necessary to reach Cameron's policy goal. Politically, the target provided frequent evidence that the government was failing to meet its own objective. More profoundly, Boswell (2015) notes that by setting such a high-profile target, the government lost the ability to distinguish between migration types, even those that receive high public support, such as students and high-skilled workers. Finally, by including EU nationals in the pledge, the government implicitly made clear that it saw the ability to control immigration of EU nationals as more important than its EU treaty obligations and that it did not regard free movement of persons as unquestionable, nor as separate or preferable to the long-term desire for balance between numbers and control. These mistakes were later repeated by Cameron in the pre-referendum renegotiation, as discussed below.

How 'EU immigration' activated latent British Euroscepticism

By 2005, in opposition, David Cameron became the Conservatives' fourth consecutive Eurosceptic leader whose only solution to 'the Europe question' was to attempt to silence his party – 'stop banging on about Europe' – for electoral expediency. This partially resulted in the rapid growth of UKIP. In 2013, Cameron as Prime Minister, and at that time struggling in the polls, promised a referendum on EU membership should his party win the 2015 general election. In doing so, the Conservatives joined Labour, the Liberal Democrats, the Scottish National Party, Plaid Cymru, the Green Party, the BNP and UKIP, all of which had made commitments to a referendum on or withdrawal from the EU at some point in the previous 40 years, justifying the country's characterisation as an 'awkward partner' of 'reluctant Europeans' (George 1998).

Mirroring and driving the political elite's latent Euroscepticism has been the even more pronounced Euroscepticism of the British electorate. Britons have consistently given a far more negative appraisal of the effect of EU membership than that of the average EU citizen. Moreover, according to the pan-EU Eurobarometer poll, Britons' had the *most* negative appraisal of the effect of the EU of any member state's electorate in 50 per cent of the years since 1973 and the most or second-most in 90 per cent (Evans *et al.* 2017). By 2009, for the first time since the period immediately after accession, the UK electorate had a net negative appraisal of the EU according to Eurobarometer data. However, public antipathy towards immigration cannot fully explain Britons' decreasingly positive perception of the EU, and eventually Brexit itself, because most of the decline in positivity to European integration came before the 2004 enlargement.

Moreover, though attitudes to European integration were increasingly negative by 2000, the salience of the topic – how important voters believed the issue was to their lives or to the country – was thereafter exceptionally low, as shown in Figure 1. After the debate over the Maastricht Treaty had subsided, British Euroscepticism became a side issue and a *passive predisposition*. Instead, aside from the most acute period of the Great Recession, the most salient issue in British politics during the twenty-first century has been immigration.

From the early 2000s onwards, the British domestic debate over Europe became almost entirely subsumed into the debate over immigration. As shown in Figure 2, non-EU annual immigration increased after 1997, from an annual average of around 150,000 to 350,000 by 2002. By this time, public concern over immigration had also begun to show a rapid increase; with over 40 per cent of Britons listing it as one of the three most important issues affecting the country on the eve of the Great Recession. Those most likely to express concern were social conservatives alarmed at the, in their view, growing heterogeneity, rootlessness and disposability that were coming to define and undermine British society, all the while becoming an integral part of the British liberal economic model. Simultaneously, lower skilled workers remained the most likely to believe that immigration – particularly of other low skilled workers – was likely to have a range of negative economic consequences on jobs for British citizens, on government accounts,

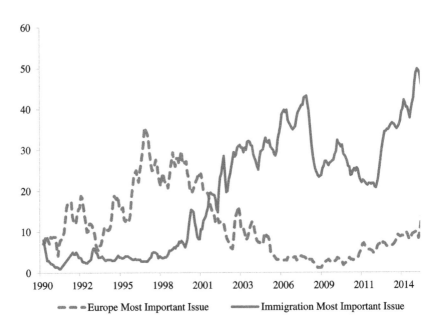

Figure 1. Percent saying Europe and immigration as one of three 'most important issues affecting the UK'. (Source: Ipsos Mori).

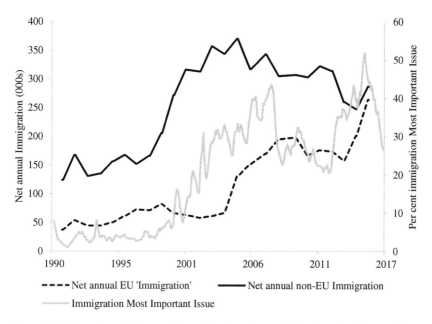

Figure 2. EU and non-EU annual net immigration and immigration issue salience. (Sources: Office of National Statistics; Ipsos Mori).

social spending and on the national and local economy more generally (Ford and Goodwin 2014). Moreover, even many centre-left political elites came to accept the idea that the necessary 'price' of liberal migration regimes was a reduction in the social rights of migrants (Ruhs 2016) and that there exists a 'progressive's dilemma' whereby high immigration rates were likely to undermine the social solidarity that legitimised high social spending, even if this idea has come under criticism (Parker 2017).

Prior to 2010, movement from other EU member states lagged behind non-EU immigration. In that year, a Conservative-led coalition government took power with the declared intention to reduce immigration. Unable to stop flows of EU citizens, the government placed more stringent controls on non-EU immigration. Simultaneously, as the UK economy came out of recession, the Eurozone crisis entered its most acute phase, further encouraging citizens from southern and eastern European member states to move to the UK rather than Eurozone countries. This, combined with the end of transitional controls on citizens of Romania and Bulgaria coming to the UK in 2013 and a relatively strong Pound Sterling, led to an uptick in movement to the UK by citizens of these countries. By 2014, movement to the UK by EU citizens had overtaken annual non-EU net migration and by 2015 it had reached nearly 350,000 per annum. Finally, it was revealed in early 2016 that the number of annual registrations by EU nationals for National Insurance – the

UK's social security scheme – had been more than double the official immigration statistics, adding to the growing sense of alarm amongst conservatives regarding the UK's immigration policy, now increasingly 'Europeanised'. One of the major attitudinal results of these changes was that the positive correlation between EU attitudes and immigration attitudes increased steadily from 2004 onwards (Evans and Mellon 2016).

After 2010, the primary electoral beneficiaries of the increased salience of immigration were UKIP who consciously and successfully pursued a strategy of fusing the immigration debate and EU membership (Goodwin and Milazzo 2015). Whereas the anti-immigration vote prior to 2010 had been split between the British National Party, UKIP and, primarily, the Conservatives, the implosion of the former and the entry of the latter into government meant that UKIP were well placed to put electoral pressure on the Conservatives (Goodwin and Dennison 2018).

Immigration in the EU referendum campaign and vote

The issue of immigration affected the campaign and vote in three ways. First, the referendum campaign was preceded by a renegotiation over the terms of the UK's membership, one of the key aims of which was to reduce the flows of EU citizens moving to the UK. Cameron had entered the negotiations aiming to ensure that EU nationals would not be able to claim in-work benefits or social housing for four years after arriving in the UK. However, such structural discrimination was plainly incompatible with single market membership, free movement, and provisions on non-discrimination. In the end, the EU attempted to get around the treaty rights by offering an 'alert and safeguard' mechanism in line with Cameron's demands but which could only be triggered if a member state could demonstrate inflows of an 'exceptional magnitude' over 'an extended period of time' undermining 'essential aspects of its social security system'. In this case, only the Commission could trigger the 'emergency brake' and it would only come into force if agreed by all heads of government in the Council. The British Eurosceptic press and many backbench Conservative MPs dismissed the renegotiation outcome as worthless. In the campaign itself, Cameron and pro-EU organisations were then forced to avoid the topic, highlighting, like Cameron's initial 'tens-of-thousands' target, the government's inability to either halt rights-based free movement while in the EU or return to the UK's historic consensus of 'balance' between functional and post-functional outcomes while an EU member.

Second, and related, the two pro-Leave campaigns – the official *Vote Leave* and the breakaway, unofficial *Leave.EU* – explicitly used anti-immigration rhetoric throughout the campaign. This was particularly the case of the more populist, less cerebral and more openly anti-immigration *Leave.EU*, which included UKIP leader Nigel Farage and many of UKIP's financiers and strategists. *Leave.EU* explicitly mimicked UKIP's prior strategy of fusing immigration and EU membership. For example, *Leave.EU* pointed out that EU proposals to allow visa-free travel to Turkish citizens had been tabled by the Commission in relation to a deal with Turkey on accommodating people displaced by the conflict in Syria, warning citizens to 'brace yourself for another influx'. The practical result of the division between two pro-Leave campaigns was that the unofficial *Leave.EU* campaign was able to do all it could to mobilise voters concerned about high immigration levels while the official *Vote Leave* campaign could take an ostensibly higher-minded position and so retain those Eurosceptics concerned with sovereignty and economic policy since the days of Maastricht and the ERM crisis (Clarke *et al.* 2017).

Third, public opinion about EU membership did not change during the campaign, unable as it was to escape the debate over immigration, about which most citizens already had strong prior views. There was almost no variation in voting intention in the EU referendum in the six months prior to the vote. Controlling for 'house' (i.e., polling company) and 'mode' (i.e., the means by which respondents were contacted) effects, Clarke *et al.* (2016) use a dynamic factor analysis to show that Leave had a consistent lead throughout the campaign of a couple of percentage points. Indeed, attitudes to EU membership had been fairly stable since 2008 and increasingly correlated with attitudes to immigration, so that, partially because of the immigration issue, few citizens changed their preferences during the EU referendum (see also British Election Study).

Ultimately, these dynamics were reflected in the vote itself in which attitudes to immigration were the major attitudinal predictor of vote choice, after attitudes to the EU itself (Clarke *et al.* 2017). British Election Study data show that Leave voters were considerably more anti-immigration than Remain voters and that 'immigration' and 'sovereignty' were the two issues most cited by Leave voters as motivations for their vote choice (Fieldhouse *et al.* 2017).

The future of EU-UK immigration policy

The Brexit vote demonstrated the fusion of concerns about European integration and immigration. The result is that the UK government will attempt to replace the rights-based EU free movement with a permission-based regime. Opponents of the EU had successfully labelled EU citizens as 'EU immigrants'. The Brexit vote means that this understanding will enter the UK legal framework as the government of Theresa May made it clear that her government would seek to end free movement as a key element of its approach to Brexit. UK governments have long prioritised control over openness, even at the price of economic success, and it is quite possible that the UK will see its economic growth slow down, or even retreat.

Perhaps the key cause of Brexit was an interaction between Britons' relatively strong latent Euroscepticism, on the one hand, and post-1992 European integration and post-2004 free movement, on the other (Evans *et al.* 2017). These issues have been reflected in the UK's primary objectives during its negotiations with the EU since the Brexit vote: first, minimising the direct jurisdiction of the EU's Court of Justice and, second, ending the right to free movement of persons, while, third, seeking to minimise economic disruption. The UK negotiating position, certainly in the immediate months after the triggering of Article 50, can be summarised, much like its constitutional arrangements, as opaque and even contradictory, as well as necessarily flexible. Its position is, to a large extent, found in assorted speeches and official statements. The first of these was Theresa May's Lancaster House speech in January 2017, which included 12 points regarding UK objectives, three of which related to immigration. First, the Common Travel Area with Ireland should be maintained. Second, free movement of persons between the UK and EU should end. Third, the rights for EU nationals currently in Britain and *vice versa* should be maintained if reciprocity could be achieved, and as speedily as possible. In these basic terms, the three objectives of the UK and EU were similar, except regarding free movement. A June 2017 Home Office document entitled 'Safeguarding the Position of EU Citizens Living in the UK and UK Nationals Living in the EU' outlined a number of policy proposals including a guaranteed right of residence and non-discrimination towards EU nationals living in the UK (labelled 'settled status') after Brexit, as well as providing the legal mechanisms for such EU citizens to obtain their new, mandatory residence status after, first, the period in which free movement applies and, second, a 'grace period' of unspecified length, to avoid a 'cliff-edge'.

A leaked UK government document in September 2017 on future immigration policy outlined a three-phase move away from rights-based free movement to a permission-based immigration system (Hopkins and Travis 2017). First, the introduction, pre-Brexit, of an Immigration Bill. Second, an implementation period during which time EU citizens moving to the UK would be required to register with the Home Office and receive a permit valid for 2 years. The third period would see EU citizens subject to the same potentially stringent controls as non-EU migrants. The government expressed a desire to encourage immigration into higher skilled employment running counter to the previous tendency in the liberal, deregulated UK labour market for EU citizens to be employed in both lower and higher skilled employment. It was expressly stated that UK employers should aim to meet their labour requirements from 'resident labour'.

The EU's position may be summarised as seeking a relationship as close to the *status quo ante* the EU referendum as possible, also to minimise disruption and losses, but with an additional aim to disincentivise additional unravelling of European integration (thus far, support for European integration has tended to increase since the EU referendum; see Evans *et al.* 2017; Paul and Aleks 2018). The EU's positions, both transparent and rigid, were established by four key documents: the European Council (Art. 50) guidelines for Brexit negotiations published in April 2017; the European Commission's 'Recommendation for a Council Decision authorising the Commission to open negotiations' published in May 2017, along with an annex; the Council's 'Negotiating Directives' published later in May; and the European Parliament resolution on negotiations from April, which the EU negotiating team was obliged to 'regard', particularly in light of the EP's veto power over the final deal. The Commission also published 'position papers' throughout the negotiations – at the time of writing there were over 20 such papers, the most relevant of which to immigration is that on 'citizens' rights'.

From this assortment of documents, the EU's negotiating position comprises three key aims. First, the Council's guidelines reaffirm that 'the four freedoms of the Single Market are indivisible and that there could be no 'cherry picking', *ergo*, the UK could not retain single market membership while ending free movement. Second, the Council highlighted the primacy of securing the maintenance of rights of EU nationals already living in the UK and *vice versa*, presumably in perpetuity, as the first priority for the negotiations. Third, the Council aimed to secure free movement, or a 'soft border', between the Republic of Ireland and Northern Ireland, whilst maintaining the integrity of the Union legal order, i.e., placing no barriers between the Republic of Ireland and the rest of the European Union. The Commission's recommendation to the Council echoed each of the three points above. The Council's Negotiating Directives went into further legal detail on citizens' rights and their legal basis. The European Parliament's resolution also echoed the three principles, as well suggesting an openness to British citizens retaining their rights as European citizens.

Following the second round of negotiations in July 2017, the Commission published a joint technical note on the UK and EU positions on Citizens' Rights and the points of 'convergence', 'divergence' and 'further discussion needed'. The former group of issues – 22 of the 44 in total – included the right of EU residents in the UK to remain, the right of their current family members to residence, as well as a number of administrative legal and terminological issues. The points of divergence – numbering 14 – included issues around health insurance, EU national posted workers, the rights of future family members, the judicial process for guaranteeing rights, a monitoring role for the Commission, rights for EU citizens with 'strong ties' to the UK, rights of EU citizen criminals to residence, voting rights, the right of UK nationals to live in just one member state or the entire EU and the exporting of benefit payments by EU citizens. Tentatively we may conclude that progress was being made towards a *withdrawal* deal on the issue of *current* residents and that doing so in time for March 2019 remained feasible though uncertain. The end of free movement in 2019 for those non-current resident EU citizens was con-firmed in a Downing Street statement in July 2017. However, one week earlier the UK Home Secretary, Amber Rudd, wrote in *The Financial Times* that the UK was looking for a highly liberal immigration regime for EU nationals after Brexit, as well as stating 'I also want to reassure businesses and EU nationals that we will ensure there is no 'cliff edge' once we leave the bloc (Rudd 2017).' Any reciprocal deal based on these terms will see UK citizens lose their right to free movement in the EU.

The eventual outcome of the Brexit negotiation will have profound effects on the UK immigration system. This system was under strain for more than 10 years in the run-up to the Brexit vote, which, in turn, highlighted the troubled relation-ship between immigration, free movement and wider concerns about the oper-ation and effects of the UK political economy. While the UK economy may have become reliant on migrant workers, there is little to suggest wider public support for relatively high levels of migration to support the continuation of such an approach. Any restrictions on future entry will hit certain sectors of the UK significantly and, at this point, the concentrated beneficiaries of a more expansive approach to labour migration, such as business groups, will need to make their case to a government that is highly attuned to the potential electoral effects of negative attitudes to immigration. The referendum exposed the debate about immigration to wider public scrutiny and, by doing so, raised more profound questions about the future shape of the British economy and the political model necessary to sustain it (see Gamble 2018).

Conclusion

It is by now well established that immigration and free movement played a key role in Britain's decision to leave the EU. In this article, we sought to move beyond this insight to also explore the meaning of the exit vote for the dynamics of migration politics and policy-making. We identify a number of key tensions in the UK's pre-Brexit migration regime: between functionalist and postfunctionalist policy making; between the historic assumptions behind UK immigration policy – notably the perceived imperative of balan-cing numbers and the capacity to integrate newcomers – and the legal con-straints of the EU; between increasing Europeanised immigration yet stubbornly non-European British self-identity; and finally between the prefer-ences of organised interests and the electorate as a whole.

We also showed that immigration did not make the United Kingdom con-siderably more Eurosceptic. Instead, the debate over Europe, which had already hardened in the UK by the late 1990s and was always more pro-nounced in both the elite and electorate than elsewhere in Europe, became fused with a public debate on immigration, which became considerably more Europeanised throughout the 2010s. This far more explosive issue transformed passive predispositions about Europe into active predictors of vote choice and party membership, giving the Conservative Prime Minister little hope of winning a general election without somehow reassuring some Eurosceptic, anti-immigration voters.

The referendum gave the general public a decisive say on the issue of Britain's future relations with the EU, but a question that remains open is the extent to which 'normal service' will be resumed during the Brexit talks. The UK government is likely to be attentive to the needs of business and it is more likely during the negotiations that the well-organised, concentrated beneficiaries of a more expansive approach to migration will mobilise and seek to exert influence. The UK cannot rapidly change the labour market model that has developed over the last 30 years and to which migrant labour has been fundamental. But with the Brexit negotiations under constant public scrutiny a new, largely immovable parameter was set by the EU referendum result that seems highly likely to lead to a decline in 'Europeanised' migration to the UK, linked both to the end of the free movement framework and a possible post-Brexit deterioration in relative British economic performance while, inevitably, there will be shocks to the labour recruitment system in key economic sectors that have become migrant reliant.

Overall, Europe's 'awkward partner' of 'reluctant Europeans' proved unable and unwilling to subordinate its desire for entirely domestic 'control' over immigration to the EU's right-based free movement of persons, let alone see fellow EU citizens in the UK as anything other than immigrants, which legally they were not. While the reasons for Brexit are primarily identitarian and post-functional, the results will test the extent to which electorates and governments are willing to put these concerns above 'bread and butter' functional concerns.

Disclosure statement

No potential conflict of interest was reported by the authors.

ORCID

James Dennison ⓘ http://orcid.org/0000-0003-3090-7124

References

Anderson, B. and Ruhs, M. (eds) (2010) *Who Needs Migrant Workers? Labour Shortages, Immigration, and Public Policy*, Oxford: Oxford University Press.

Boswell, C. (2015) 'The net migration target may have failed but it shifted the way we debate immigration', LSE British Politics and Policy blog, November 28 2015.

Bulmer, S.J. and Radaelli, C.M. (2004) 'The Europeanisation of national policy?', *Queens Papers on Europeanisation No. 42*, Queens University Belfast.

Carmel, E., Cerami, A. and Papadopoulos, T. (eds) (2011) *Migration and Welfare in the New Europe: Social Protection and the Challenges of Integration*, Bristol: Policy Press.

Clarke, H., Goodwin, M. and Whiteley, P. (2016) 'Leave was always in the lead: why the polls got the referendum result wrong', LSE British Politics and Policy, published online.

Clarke, H., Goodwin, M. and Whiteley, P. (2017) *Brexit: Why Britain Voted to Leave the EU*, Cambridge: Cambridge University Press.

Deutsch, K.W., *et al.* (1957). *Political Community and the North Atlantic Area*, New York: Greenwood Press.

ESS Round 8: European Social Survey Round 8 Data (2016) Data file edition 1.0. NSD - Norwegian Centre for Research Data, Norway – Data Archive and distributor of ESS data for ESS ERIC.

Eurobarometer 86.2 (2016) TNS opinion, Brussels [producer]. GESIS Data Archive, Cologne. ZA6788 Data file Version 1.3.0

Evans, G., Carl, N. and Dennison, J. (2017) 'Brexit: the causes and consequences of the UK's decision to leave the EU', in M. Castells, O. Bouin, J. Caraca, G. Cardoso, J. Thompson and M. Wieviorka (eds.), *Europe's Crises*, Cambridge: Polity, pp. 380–404.

Evans, G. and J. Mellon (2016) 'How immigration became a Eurosceptic issue', *LSE Brexit Blog*, available at http://blogs.lse.ac.uk/brexit/2016/01/05/how-immigration-became-a-eurosceptic-issue/ (accessed 29 August 2017).

Favell, A. (1998) *Philosophies of Integration: Immigration and the Idea of Citizenship in France and Britain*, Basingstoke: Macmillan.

Favell, A. and Barbulescu, R. (2018) 'Brexit, "immigration" and anti-discrimination', in P. Diamond, P. Nedergaard and Be. Rosamond (eds.), *The Routledge Handbook of the Politics of Brexit*, London: Routledge, forthcoming.

Favell, A., Recchi, E., Kuhn, T., Jensen, J.S. and Klein, J. (2011) 'The Europeanisation of everyday life: cross-border practices and transational identifications among EU and third-country citizens: state of the art report'. *EUCROSS Working # 1*, available at https://pure.au.dk/ws/files/53643017/EUCROSS_D2.1_State_of_the_Art.pdf (accessed 22 November 2017).

Fieldhouse, E., *et al.* (2017) 'British election study internet panel waves 1–13'. doi:10. 15127/1.293723

Ford, R. and Goodwin, M. (2014) *Revolt on the Right: Explaining Support for the Radical Right in Britain*, London: Routledge.

Ford, R., Jennings, W. and Somerville, W. (2015) 'Public opinion, responsiveness and constraint: britain's three immigration policy regimes', *Journal of Ethnic and Migration Studies* 41(9): 1391–411.

Freeman, G. (1995) 'Modes of immigration politics in liberal democratic states', *International Migration Review* 29(4): 881–902.

Gamble, A. (2018) 'Taking Back Control: The political implications of Brexit', *Journal of European Public Policy*, doi:10.1080/13501763.2018.1467952.

Geddes, A. and Scholten, P. (2016) *The Politics of Migration and Immigration in Europe*, London: Sage.

George, S. (1998) *An Awkward Partner: Britain in the European Community*, Oxford: Oxford University Press.

Goodwin, M. and Dennison, J. (2018) 'The radical right in the UK', in J. Rydgren (ed.), *The Oxford Handbook of the Radical Right*, Oxford: Oxford University Press, pp. 521–544.

Goodwin, M. and Milazzo, C. (2015) *UKIP: Inside the Campaign to Redraw the Map of British Politics*, Oxford, New York: Oxford University Press.

Hooghe, L. and Marks, G. (2009) 'A postfunctionalist theory of European integration: from permissive consensus to constraining dissensus', *British Journal of Political Science* 39(1): 1–23.

Hopkins, N. and Travis, A. (2017) 'Leaked document reveals UK Brexit plans to deter EU immigrants', *The Guardian*, 5 September, available at https://www.theguardian.com/uk-news/2017/sep/05/leaked-document-reveals-uk-brexit-plan-to-deter-eu-immigrants (accessed 30 November 2017).

Kuhn, T. (2011) 'Individual transnationalism, globalisation and euroscepticism: an empirical test of Deutsch's transactionalist theory', *European Journal of Political Research* 50(6): 811–37

Mair, P. (2014) 'Representative versus responsible government', in P. Mair (ed.), *On Parties, Party Systems and Democracy*, Colchester: ECPR Press, pp. 581–96.

Parker, O. (2017) 'Critical political economy, free movement and Brexit: beyond the progressive's dilemma', *The British Journal of Politics and International Relations* 19(3): 479–96.

Paul and Aleks (2018), 'Putting Brexit into Perspective: The effect of the Eurozone and Migration Crises and Brexit on Euroscepticism in European states', *Journal of European Public Policy*, doi:10.1080/13501763.2018.1467955

Rudd, A. (2017) 'A post-Brexit immigration system that works for all', *Financial Times*, available at https://www.ft.com/content/34228da8-7204-11e7-93ff-99f383b09ff9 (accessed 30 November 2017).

Ruhs, M. (2016) *The Price of Rights: Regulating International Labor Rights*, Princeton: Princeton University Press

Sobolewska, M., Galandini, S. and Lessard-Phillips, L. (2016) 'The public view of immigrant intengration: multidimensional and consensual. Evidence from survey experiments in the UK and the Netherlands', *Journal of Ethnic and Migration Studies* 43(1): 58–79.

Brexit: differentiated disintegration in the European Union

Frank Schimmelfennig [ID]

ABSTRACT
The decision of the Cameron government to renegotiate the terms of UK membership and to hold an in-out referendum has triggered a novel process in European integration: differentiated disintegration, the selective reduction of a member state's level and scope of integration. The article starts from an established postfunctionalist explanation of differentiated integration and claims that it also explains demand for disintegration. In this perspective, Brexit resulted from a mix of integration effects (immigration) challenging self-determination, the rise of a Eurosceptic party, and the availability of referendums. By contrast, the institutional and material bargaining power of states demanding disintegration is considerably lower than that of states demanding opt-outs in the context of integration negotiations. Consequently, demanders of disintegration moderate their demands and make concessions to the EU in the course of negotiations. The ongoing UK-EU disintegration negotiations confirm this expectation.

Introduction

In January 2013, British Prime Minister David Cameron promised to renegotiate the United Kingdom's (UK's) European integration and put its European Union (EU) membership to a referendum. This announcement triggered a novel process in the history of European integration: differentiated disintegration. This article theorizes – and explains Brexit as a case of – differentiated disintegration.

Differentiated disintegration is the selective reduction of a state's level and scope of integration. Disintegration can lead to internal differentiation if a member state remains in the EU but exits from specific policies, or external differentiation if it exits from the EU but continues to participate in selected EU policies. After Cameron's re-election in 2015, he first negotiated to consolidate and expand the UK's exemptions from EU policies as a member state; after the Brexit referendum of 23 June 2016, negotiations shifted to external differentiation.

Differentiated disintegration brings up the same research questions as the study of (differentiated) integration. First, how can we explain the British demand for disintegration, the post-Brexit arrangement the British government aims to achieve, and the negotiating positions of the other member states? Second, how can we account for the negotiating process and its outcomes? In principle, explanations of differentiated integration (e.g., Kölliker 2006; Leuffen *et al.* 2013; Schimmelfennig and Winzen 2014) may explain differentiated *dis*integration, too. Yet, authors who have recently explored disintegration theoretically have questioned the suitability of existing integration theories (Webber 2014) and cautioned against simply turning explanations of integration upside down to explain disintegration (Vollaard 2014).

This article explores whether established explanations of differentiated integration also account for Brexit, a process of differentiated disintegration. My theoretical starting point is a postfunctionalist explanation of differentiated integration, which has been corroborated in analyses of negotiations on treaty revisions (Schimmelfennig and Winzen 2014; Winzen and Schimmelfennig 2016). According to this explanation, demand for opt-outs arise from concerns about the preservation of national sovereignty in areas of core state powers and in countries with strong exclusive national identities. Thanks to their institutional bargaining power in negotiations on the deepening of European integration, Eurosceptic governments can easily attain these opt-outs. This explanation fits the history of British differentiated integration well.

This postfunctionalist explanation also applies to the demand for the UK's differentiated disintegration. Unanticipated integration outcomes in an area of core state powers – immigration – fuelled the rise of a Eurosceptic party, UKIP. The aim of reining in both UKIP and the Eurosceptic wing of the Conservative Party explain the referendum promise. Concerns about immigration and sovereignty dominated the campaign and the vote choices of the Leave camp. The preference of the May government for a 'hard Brexit' is oriented towards these concerns.

By contrast, the constellation of intergovernmental bargaining power changes fundamentally when negotiations shift from integration to disintegration. Because the UK and the remaining member states switch their positions relative to the status quo, the institutional bargaining power of status-quo actors now accrues to the EU. Material bargaining power deriving from asymmetrical interdependence works in the EU's favour, too. Finally, supranational actors and procedures affect negotiations on disintegration. We should therefore expect the UK to soften its demand for disintegration and accommodate EU preferences in the course of Brexit negotiations. Until the summer of 2017, the postfunctional logic has clearly dominated UK behaviour. Since then, however, we have seen a series of British concessions resulting from EU bargaining power.

The remainder of the article has four sections and a conclusion. The next section presents the theoretical argument. I then examine the demand for Brexit, negotiations on a new UK settlement within the EU, and the withdrawal negotiations.

Theorizing differentiated disintegration

Differentiated disintegration

Uniformity/differentiation and integration/disintegration are conceptually independent dimensions of European integration (Figure 1). Integration refers to an increase – and disintegration to a reduction – in the centralization level, policy scope, and membership of the EU (cf. Börzel 2005; Leuffen *et al.* 2013: 8). Integration and disintegration are uniform if these increases or decreases apply to all states equally (upper and lower right quadrant).

Differentiated integration is a process of unequal integration growth (upper left quadrant): Whereas the level, scope, or membership of the EU increase overall, individual states do not (fully) participate. Conversely, differentiated disintegration is a process of unequal reduction in the level, scope, or membership of the EU. The Brexit negotiations are not about a uniform 'repatriation' of EU competences, but only affect the UK. Moreover, the British government does not seek to cut ties with the EU entirely but wishes to maintain a free-trade area and privileged market access in specific sectors.

In addition, differentiation can be internal or external. Internal differentiation is differentiation among member states of the EU, whereas external differentiation refers to the selective participation of non-members in the EU's integrated policies (as in the European Economic Area). The EU-UK

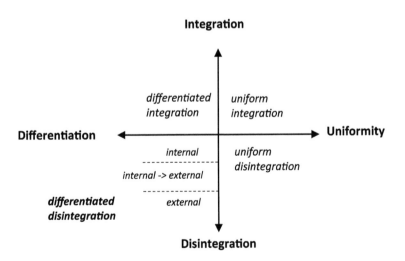

Figure 1. Differentiated disintegration.

negotiations on differentiated disintegration have consisted of two stages. Between November 2015 and February 2016, negotiations on the New Settlement for the UK within the EU concerned internal differentiated disintegration. After the negative Brexit referendum of June 2016, negotiations have focused on the UK's withdrawal from the EU and its selective integration as a non-member state (moving from internal to external differentiated disintegration). Finally, non-member states may wish to reduce their EU integration as well (external differentiated disintegration) – as in Switzerland's attempt to renegotiate the freedom of movement treaty following the 2014 Mass Immigration Initiative.

These conceptual distinctions are theoretically relevant. As I will argue below, the intergovernmental bargaining constellation varies considerably between negotiations on differentiated integration and disintegration. As a starting point, however, I will summarize the established explanation of differentiated integration in EU treaty revisions.

Differentiated integration in EU treaty revisions

The major sources of differentiated integration among the member states are 'widening', the expansion of the EU's membership, and 'deepening', the progressive delegation of state competencies to the EU and its supranational organizations. Recent research has shown that differentiated integration originating in deepening responds to member state concerns about the protection of national sovereignty and identity in an 'ever closer union' and has led to an enduring core-periphery divide (Schimmelfennig and Winzen 2014). Demand for differentiated integration is, first, most likely to arise if the EU expands its policy scope into, or deepens its supranational competences in, core state powers. Genschel and Jachtenfuchs (2014: 10) define 'core state powers' (such as a state's army, police and justice system, currency, or public administration) as those functions and policies that have particularly strong 'institutional significance for state building' and are thus closely linked to sovereignty.

Second, demand for differentiated integration is prone to be strong in member states with widespread exclusive national identities. Exclusive national identities increase the salience of sovereignty transfers and reduce support for European integration (Carey 2002; Hooghe and Marks 2005). Eurosceptic parties on the right mobilize national identities against the deepening of integration. This mobilization puts the domestic ratification of treaty revisions at risk, especially in the case of referendums on European integration. If the ratification of European treaties is in danger, governments of Eurosceptic member states can request opt-outs from the controversial policies in order to secure domestic support.

Additionally, Winzen and Schimmelfennig (2016: 631) find that wealthier member states are more likely to gain opt-outs from treaty revisions.

Wealthier states are more reluctant to integrate deeply for fear of redistribution (Beramendi 2012) or out of concern that deep integration with poorer countries might undermine their governance capacity and efficiency. Moreover, wealthier countries can better afford to refuse deeper integration than countries that benefit from EU transfers (Schimmelfennig 2016: 795).

In sum, the differentiated deepening of European integration follows the general expectation of postfunctionalist integration theory: 'To the extent that exclusive identity infuses preferences and to the extent that European issues are politicized, [...] we expect to see downward pressure on the level and scope of integration' (Hooghe and Marks 2009: 22). Such downward pressure can manifest itself in stagnation, differentiated integration and, ultimately, disintegration.

The UK's differentiated integration in the EU fits the postfunctionalist explanation well. According to the Eurobarometer surveys, the British traditionally have by far the strongest exclusive national identity among all member societies of the EU. Since the 1990s, on average over 60 percent of British respondents have expressed that they identify themselves with their 'nationality only'. When the EU began to expand its policy scope into core state powers, the UK became the champion of differentiated integration (together with Denmark). It did not join the Schengen free-travel regime and secured opt-outs from the euro, the Social Chapter of the Maastricht Treaty, the Charter of Fundamental Rights as well as from parts of the Justice and Home Affairs acquis. With the exception of the opt-out from the Social Chapter, repealed by the Blair government in 1997, the British opt-outs are in the area of core state powers and the major ones have been in force for 20 years or more.

The UK has been capable of securing so many opt-outs because of the strong institutional bargaining power that status quo-oriented member states enjoy in treaty negotiations on further integration. EU treaty revisions generally require unanimous agreement and national ratification in each member state to enter into force. That makes each government, each national parliament, and – in cases of ratification by referendum – each national electorate a veto player. In particular, unanimity strengthens the bargaining power of actors with preferences close to the integration status quo. They are the first to threaten their veto against far-reaching integration proposals and are thus able to keep reforms close to their ideal points.

Without the option of differentiated integration, integration agreements would not go beyond the preference of the most status quo-oriented member state. With the option of differentiated integration, integration can move further ahead. For one, status quo-oriented states may obtain an opt-out in return for waiving their veto. The British opt-out from monetary union is the typical example. If the status quo state is not willing to waive its veto, the other member states may conclude an intergovernmental treaty outside the EU. This happened with the Schengen Agreement in 1985 and the Fiscal Compact in 2011. Either way, status quo-oriented member states are able to realize their demand for self-determination thanks to institutional bargaining power. As we move from differentiated integration to differentiated disintegration, however, both demand and supply shift from the defence to the revision of the status quo.

From differentiated integration to differentiated disintegration

Why would a country turn from a defender of the integration status quo to an advocate of disintegration? In keeping with the explanation of demand for differentiated integration, I turn to postfunctionalism. Generally, postfunctionalism attributes differentiated integration and disintegration to a politicization process, which shifts European integration issues from the arena of interest group politics to the arena of mass politics, where the 'identity logic' of politics has a larger role (Hooghe and Marks 2009: 8). Postfunctionalism proposes several factors that may drive this shift, alone or in combination: the depth of integration, exclusive national identity, the rise of Eurosceptic parties and referendums on the EU. Moreover, in order to explain disintegration rather than simply resistance to more integration, there has to be a significant increase in these factors.

For one, disintegration could result from a strengthening of exclusive national identities. Yet Hooghe and Marks show that there has not been any discernible trend in these attitudes and largely dismiss this factor (2009: 12). Alternatively, increases in the scope and depth of integration may trigger politicization (Hooghe and Marks 2009: 13). Even when states use differentiated integration to prevent undesired deepening, European integration might produce unanticipated and unintended effects. If such 'spillovers' affect identities or core state powers, they are likely to politicize European integration and create a backlash. Moreover, the strengthening of political entrepreneurs, especially populist right-wing parties, who mobilize Eurosceptic attitudes, may boost demand for disintegration (Hooghe and Marks 2009: 13, 18). Finally, a higher availability or use of referendums on European integration opens an institutional venue for disintegration demand (Hooghe and Marks 2009: 18).

Thus, based on postfunctionalism, I hypothesize that *demand for disintegration increases with (a) the spillover of integration into identity-relevant areas; (b) the rise of Eurosceptic parties; and (c) an increase in the availability or use of referendums on European integration.*

How does the supply side change when demand for disintegration replaces opposition to deepened integration? Three factors are relevant for disintegration negotiations: distance to the status quo, supranational institutional factors, and material bargaining power. Most fundamentally, the

Eurosceptic state and the rest of the EU switch their institutional bargaining positions. Whereas integration-friendly states become the defenders of the status quo, the Eurosceptic state demands its revision and loses the power that EU rules of treaty change confer upon status quo defenders. Rather, the member state that is most negatively affected by, and thus most adverse to, disintegration defines the limits of treaty change.

In addition, supranational institutional factors work to the disadvantage of the state demanding disintegration. Supranational institutions are weaker in integration negotiations, at the end of which states create or strengthen institutions, than in negotiations on disintegration, in which institutions are already present and entrenched. In addition, supranational actors have a vested institutional interest in defending the status quo against disintegration – and are powerful if they obtain a formal role in the disintegration procedure.

Finally, the demanders of disintegration typically find themselves in a situation of inferior material bargaining power. The market size and the related economic power of any single member state is small in comparison with the EU as a whole. Moreover, for each individual member state, the importance of being in the single market normally exceeds the importance of alternative economic relations. Neither the global market nor other regional markets can compensate the loss of access to the EU market. This is also true of the UK, even though it is one of the largest, economically strongest, and most globally oriented member states. In 2015, 44 percent of UK exports (goods and services) went to the EU and 53 percent of UK imports came from the EU. By contrast, the UK only accounted for 6–7 percent of EU exports and 4–5 percent of EU imports.[1] Given the geographical proximity, the EU will remain the UK's most important foreign market.

This asymmetrical material interdependence looms less large in negotiations of differentiated integration than in negotiations on differentiated disintegration. States that reject further integration forgo the gains that more integration might provide but they do not risk their existing benefits. As a result, they can credibly threaten the other member states with non-cooperation. By contrast, states that demand disintegration cannot credibly threaten the EU with no or outside agreements because such threats would turn them into net losers and inflict higher losses on themselves than on the EU.

There are three basic types of differentiated disintegration. For one, a state may seek shallower integration within the EU (internal differentiation). Because an opt-out from existing integration requires the unanimous agreement of all other member states, such agreement will only obtain under the condition that renegotiation does not have significant negative effects for other member states or the Union as a whole. Yet most often demand for differentiated disintegration stems exactly from the desire to privilege and protect domestic firms and citizens and to reduce national contributions to integrated policies. It is in the collective interest of the member states to protect the integrity of the integration project from the proliferation of such free-riding or cherry-picking behaviour.

If a member state is refused internal disintegration, it may want to exit from the EU (move from internal to external differentiation). The main difference is that, under Article 50 of the Treaty on European Union, the other member states cannot legally stop disintegration. Whereas the non-agreement outcome in internal disintegration is the status quo, it is 'no integration' in the case of exit. Yet Article 50 accords the remaining states an institutionally favourable position to determine the terms of withdrawal and the future relationship. First, the exiting state negotiates with the EU as a whole, represented by the European Commission. This procedure strengthens the unity and bargaining power of the EU. Second, the withdrawal agreement requires the consent of the European Parliament. Third, Article 50 negotiations are limited to two years. Only unanimous agreement of the remaining member states can extend the negotiating period. Fourth, any treaty on the future relationship going beyond a basic (free) trade agreement is a 'mixed agreement' requiring national ratification in all member states. The institutional provisions of the Article 50 procedure thus make it difficult for the exiting state to break the lines of the remaining member states. If the exiting state rejects a withdrawal settlement and a future relationship that is acceptable to the remaining member states, it leaves the EU without any agreement at all – the most materially detrimental outcome.

Finally, a selectively integrated non-member state may demand a shallower integration outside the EU (external differentiation). In this context, the difference between negotiating differentiated integration and disintegration is less stark than for member states because non-members are generally in a weak institutional and material bargaining position. Non-member states cannot prevent the EU from moving ahead with integration, always negotiate with the EU as a whole, and require the unanimous agreement of the member states for both increasing and decreasing their selective integration.

In sum, demand and supply conditions are inconsistent in the process of differentiated disintegration. Strong domestic political demand for disintegration translates into a weak institutional and material international bargaining position. Unitary, economically rational, and fully informed actors are therefore likely to refrain from disintegration in the first place – or make only moderate demands. Yet postfunctionalism assumes a split between elites and masses, identity-driven behaviour, and – potentially – weakly informed citizens getting a say through referendums. I therefore formulate a supply-side hypothesis that assumes a learning process: *States demanding differentiated disintegration from the EU moderate their demands and make concessions to the EU in the course of disintegration negotiations.* In the following sections, I apply the demand-side and supply-side hypotheses to the UK demand for differentiated disintegration and the UK-EU negotiations.

The demand for Brexit

All three factors hypothesized to generate demand for disintegration were present in the run-up to the Brexit vote. The internal market and the Eastern enlargement of the EU gave an unanticipated and undesired boost to immigration to the UK. The right-wing Eurosceptic United Kingdom Independence Party (UKIP) strengthened its role in British politics and scored important electoral successes. Finally, David Cameron announced a referendum on membership to placate Eurosceptics in his own Conservative Party and counter the electoral threat of UKIP.

Whereas the UK has regularly opposed the transfer of core state powers to the EU, it has always been an ardent supporter of the internal market and enlargement. And whereas it has regularly sought opt-outs from treaty revisions, it was one of only four member states opening its labour market to the ten new member states in 2004. Thanks to its liberal immigration policy and economic attractiveness, the UK has seen an increase in net migration since the late 1990s. This net migration has initially originated from outside the EU – and has remained a predominantly non-EU phenomenon. Yet the share of net migration from the EU has risen since the mid-2000s, first after Eastern enlargement and then again because of the Great Recession.[2] Immigration from the EU has been an effect of British advocacy for deep and wide European market integration, but British governments neither intended nor anticipated its size and growth. Consequently, both major parties have abandoned their liberal immigration policy stances. Yet intra-EU migration is guaranteed as an individual right by the EU's freedom of movement rules. Despite its pledge to bring down immigration significantly to the 'tens of thousands', the Conservative government failed to do so ahead of the Brexit vote. In a YouGov survey at the end of 2015, 63 percent of the respondents named immigration as the most pressing issue facing Britain – giving it a 24-percentage point lead over healthcare, the second issue (Clarke *et al.* 2017: 11). The discrepancy between issue salience and government performance was ready for exploitation by a challenger party.

This is what UKIP did. The party combined its traditional Europhobia with 'strident opposition to mass immigration and the free movement of EU nationals. The dual strategy of communicating both anti-EU and anti-immigration messages was accompanied by populist attacks against the established parties' (Clarke *et al.* 2017: 88). This formula resonated well with voters and carried UKIP to electoral success, above all in the 2014 European elections (Clarke *et al.* 2017: 111–45). In addition, UKIP infused the EU membership issue with the salience of the immigration issue and the dissatisfaction with government performance and thus put powerful momentum behind the Leave campaign.

Since the 1975 EU referendum, direct democratic mechanisms had not driven or constrained British EU policy. In contrast to Denmark, the other champion of differentiated integration, none of the British opt-outs resulted from negative referendums. Rather, UK governments secured differentiated integration in negotiations ahead of intergovernmental agreement. Yet, the Europe-wide divide between more integration-friendly political and economic elites and sceptical citizens applies to the UK as well. Introducing referendums on European integration was therefore bound to increase the chances of differentiated integration or even disintegration.

Cameron agreed to give referendums a greater role in the (vain) hope to appease EU opponents inside his own party and deflect the UKIP challenge (Bale 2016; Menon and Salter 2016; Wellings and Vines 2016). When he was opposition leader, Cameron vowed to put any new treaty to a referendum (Armstrong 2017: 24–5). This demand found its way into the 'referendum lock' of the European Union Act of 2011. Nevertheless, 81 Conservative MPs supported a bill for an in-out referendum, defying a three-line whip, in the same year. With Eurosceptic Conservatives continuing to push for a referendum on membership and UKIP rising, Cameron promised in his January 2013 Bloomberg speech to negotiate a new settlement for the UK in the EU, to be followed by an in-out referendum before the end of 2017. Initially, the referendum pledge bought Cameron time – but he had to make good on his promise after leading the Conservatives to victory in the 2015 general elections.

Thus, all postfunctionalist ingredients of disintegration were in place: identity-challenging feedback effects of integration (Dennison and Geddes 2018), a non-mainstream party seizing on these effects and mobilizing voters, and the creation of an institutional (referendum) venue. These conditions are best seen as necessary enabling conditions. Without the rise and salience of immigration, UKIP mobilization, and Cameron agreeing to an in-out referendum, it is hard to imagine how Brexit could have happened.

The referendum campaign and outcome further support the postfunctionalist explanation. The Leave campaign focused on issues of identity and self-determination. It vowed to 'take back control' in order to limit immigration and the economic, cultural, and security threats it posed, to restore sovereignty and democracy, and to redirect financial contributions from the EU to the UK (Clarke *et al.* 2017: 59–60). Accordingly, voters who believed that Britain would be better able to control immigration and prevent terrorism outside the EU were significantly more likely to vote for Leave (Clarke *et al.* 2017: 161–5). By contrast, the Remain campaign focused on the negative economic consequences of Brexit. Economists from international organizations such as the OECD and the IMF, the British Treasury, think tanks, and private consultancies were in almost full agreement about the harm that

Brexit would inflict on the UK economy. In addition, the UK business community and its major interest groups were overwhelmingly in favour of remaining in the EU and its single market (Jensen and Snaith 2016: 1304–5). In line with the campaign, voters who thought that Britain would be economically worse off and lose international influence if it left the EU, and that Brexit generally entailed high risks, were significantly more likely to vote to remain (Clarke *et al.* 2017: 161–5).

Finally, Remain and Leave voters reflected the divide between and elites and masses and the cleavage between cultural and economic integration winners and losers that postfunctionalism assumes. Pro-Brexit voters were older, poorer, less educated, more socially and culturally conservative, and more rural than anti-Brexit voters (Hobolt 2016); they had more negative attitudes towards immigration, considered the UK to have lost control of its economy, perceived themselves as 'left behind', and were more likely to identify as English (Clarke *et al.* 2017: 166–170).

Before the referendum: negotiating internal differentiated disintegration

Prime Minister Cameron linked his referendum announcement to negotiations of a new settlement for the UK within the EU. Depending on their outcome, he would either recommend voters to leave or remain. In principle, this linkage promised two advantages. First, he could use the threat of a negative recommendation and a negative referendum to extract concessions from the other member states. Second, by extracting concessions, he would improve his chances to convince undecided voters and moderate Eurosceptics to vote for Remain.

Yet it was clear that Cameron preferred the UK to be in the EU and that he had called the referendum to fend off domestic political pressure, not to pave the way for Brexit. It was also not in his interest to push for concessions he knew the EU would not make and thereby force him to make a negative recommendation against his own will.

The threat of a negative referendum outcome depended on two further parameters. First, how negatively did the other member states assess a potential British exit from the EU? Second, how likely was it in their opinion that the British would actually vote to leave? Apart from a survey of national think tank experts on the positions and debates in their countries (Möller and Oliver 2014; Oliver 2015, 2016), there is little evidence to answer these questions systematically, however.

According to the survey, the other member states had different interests in the UK's EU membership, which ranged from the economic, security and geopolitical importance of Britain to the relevance of the UK for the internal EU balance of interests and power. For all their different interests, however, the other member states converged on a common preference to have Britain in rather than out. At the same time, member states generally agreed that British membership was not the most important issue on the EU agenda and that their primary commitment was to the EU. There was little sympathy for British 'negative leadership', 'spoiler' and 'bystander' roles, for its 'pick-and-choose' policies, or for its threat-based negotiation behaviour (Möller and Oliver 2014: 104, 106; Oliver 2016).

The survey does not contain information on international perceptions of how likely Brexit was. It is plausible to assume, however, that the governments of the other member states shared the view of the British government and the overwhelming elite and expert opinion that the electorate would shy away from the risks of Brexit at the end of the day (Clarke *et al.* 2017: 3).

In sum, the credibility of Cameron's referendum threat was low. Because both Cameron and the EU had an interest in the UK remaining a member, and assuming that both expected a positive referendum outcome, Cameron would only ask for, and the EU would only be willing to make, moderate concessions. Given their interest in Cameron winning the referendum, the other member states would give him something to show at home. At the same time, the secondary importance of the Brexit issue and the low sympathy for the UK reform positions and approach in most member states would make major concessions unlikely. The negotiations on the 'new settlement' and their outcomes are in line with these expectations.

In his November 2015 letter to Donald Tusk, President of the European Council, Cameron proposed reforms that amounted to a general confirmation and moderate expansion of Britain's differentiated integration in the EU.[3] In the area of economic governance, Cameron was 'not seeking a new opt-out for the UK'. Rather, he proposed a series of safeguards against negative consequences of Euro-area policies for non-Euro area countries. In the area of sovereignty, he sought a legally binding opt-out from the treaty obligation to 'ever closer union' and continuing UK discretion with regard to participation in Justice and Home Affairs policies.

Finally, in the area of immigration, he put forward measures to limit the free movement for citizens of *future* new member states, to fight the abuse of free movement, to restrict in-work benefits to EU citizens for a period of four years, and to end the sending of child benefit payments overseas. This is the only area in which Cameron clearly demanded differentiated disintegration, which would exempt Britain from existing treaty obligations and discriminate against current and future member states. At the same time, Cameron knew that most member states considered a general opt-out from the freedom of movement non-negotiable (Weiss and Blockmans 2016: 9). Although it was his goal to reduce immigration from the EU, he did not even ask for direct measures such as quota or a 'point system' but focused on temporary and indirect measures.

In their report, Weiss and Blockmans characterize the negotiations as driven by the 'fundamental desire' to reach agreement (2016: 1). The EU could easily accept those proposals that did not go beyond an affirmation and consolidation of the status quo of differentiated integration – as in the areas of economic governance and sovereignty. On the contested issue of financial market regulation in the context of the new banking union, the European Council Decision remained vague. While pointing to the need to apply the Single Rulebook to all member states 'to ensure the level-playing field within the internal market', it also conceded that rules for Eurozone countries 'may need to be conceived in a more uniform manner' than those of non-Eurozone countries (European Council 2016). Yet a UK veto against decisions of the banking union and Eurozone was rejected from the start (Weiss and Blockmans 2016: 5).

EU concessions in the area of sovereignty were mainly symbolic. Even though some integration-friendly member states objected to the formal weakening of the principle of 'ever closer union', the EU merely acknowledged established practice. The European Council reiterated a passage from its June 2014 conclusions noting that 'the concept of ever closer union allows for different paths of integration for different member states' (European Council 2014). It further stated that 'the references to ever closer union do not apply to the United Kingdom', affirmed that powers could be returned to the member states, and clarified that the principle did not provide a legal basis for the informal expansion of EU competences (European Council 2016).

Unsurprisingly, the most contested area was immigration. In contrast to the other areas, it involved demands for disintegration and mattered strongly for UK voters. It was not surprising either that the strongest opposition came from the new member states whose citizens benefited most from the freedom of movement to the UK. Yet the integrity of the internal market was a fundamental principle for all member states (Weiss and Blockmans 2016: 9). In the end, the EU decided to accommodate British concerns without granting the UK differentiated disintegration. The agreed measures, an 'emergency brake' for in-work benefits and the indexing of child benefits, affected secondary legislation but not the treaties. They applied to all member states and not just the UK; and they were exceptional and conditional measures decided collectively (rather than by the UK alone). In sum, the negotiations consolidated but did not change the landscape of differentiated integration. In the absence of a perceived credible UK threat, the outcome fell short of internal differentiated disintegration.

After the referendum: moving from internal to external differentiation

The victory of Leave in the referendum mandated the new Prime Minister Theresa May to take the UK out of the EU, but it did not prescribe any specific non-membership arrangement. The two essential options turned out to be 'soft Brexit', which would keep the UK in the internal market or at least in a customs union with the EU, and 'hard Brexit', which would result in a free-trade and sectoral cooperation agreement.

After months of vagueness ('Brexit means Brexit'), May came out in favour of a 'hard Brexit' in her Lancaster House speech in January 2017, an option she confirmed in her withdrawal letter to the EU. May excluded membership in the internal market, which would mean accepting EU legislation, the jurisdiction of the Court of Justice (CJEU), the freedom of movement for labour, and 'vast contributions' to the EU budget. She also vowed to pull out of the customs union that prevents the UK from concluding its own trade agreements. At the same time, the UK would seek 'the greatest possible access' to the internal market through a 'new, comprehensive, bold and ambitious free-trade arrangement'.[4] In her withdrawal letter of 29 March 2017, May spoke of a 'deep and special partnership', taking in 'both economic and security cooperation' and a free-trade agreement that would also cover areas 'crucial to our linked economies such as financial services and network industries', i.e., the two sectors that would suffer most from the UK's exit from the internal market.[5]

This initial, pre-negotiation position gave clear priority to the postfunctional aim of restoring sovereignty and limiting immigration. 'Greatest possible access' was understood as greatest access without compromising formal sovereignty. In her notification letter, May characterized the referendum as 'a vote to restore ... our national self-determination'.[6] The 'hard Brexit' option followed the priorities of the Leave campaign as well as the Tory voters. Although the British public generally preferred a solution that would allow the UK to maintain market access to the EU and regain control of immigration at the same time, when faced with the trade-off, voters of the Conservative Party prioritized migration control by 60:40 percent.[7]

By contrast, the EU's negotiating positions reflect the aims of preserving the unity and integrity of the EU and its supranational rules and institutions. In its Guidelines, the European Council (2017) emphasized the 'integrity of the Single Market'. It ruled out a 'sector-by-sector approach' and called for a level playing field in terms of state aid and competition. Procedurally, the EU rejected separate, bilateral negotiations with the UK in favour of a 'single package' and a 'single channel of communication'. Importantly, it demanded a 'phased approach to negotiations', starting with agreement on the terms of withdrawal and moving to negotiations on the future agreement only after 'sufficient progress has been achieved'. 'Transitional arrangements' to bridge the temporal gap between the end of the Article 50 negotiation period and the entry into force of a new agreement with the UK would be limited in time and governed by EU rules.

In the first phase, the Union pursued three priorities: a guarantee of the existing rights of EU citizens in the UK enforced by the Court of Justice of the EU (CJEU); a 'single financial settlement' covering the UK's financial obligations towards and assets in the EU; and the avoidance of a 'hard border' in Ireland. In principle, May's notification letter agreed to these three priorities. Yet she proposed negotiating the terms of the future partnership 'alongside those of our withdrawal' rather than afterwards.[8] Her government also expected that it would be possible to conclude a new agreement within the two years of Brexit negotiations, and it rejected any post-Brexit CJEU jurisdiction (except for ongoing cases) or payments into the EU budget.[9]

In order to bolster their negotiating positions, both sides exchanged threats. May asserted repeatedly that 'no deal was better than a bad deal' for Britain. Moreover, the UK government threatened the EU with downgrading security and intelligence cooperation and with aggressive tax and regulatory competition.[10] On its part, the EU repeatedly warned the UK that it would not negotiate a future partnership unless the UK agreed to its terms of withdrawal – and dismissed the 'no deal' threat as lacking credibility.[11]

The record of the negotiation process and the intermediate agreements confirm the expectation that, owing to asymmetrical interdependence and inferior material and institutional bargaining power, the UK would make asymmetrical concessions to the EU. Already in the first round of negotiations, the UK accepted the phased approach of the withdrawal negotiations.[12] Ahead of the second round, Brexit minister Davis acknowledged that the UK would have to settle financial obligations toward the EU. In her Florence speech of 22 September 2017, Prime Minister May pledged to 'honour commitments we have made during the period of our membership' and that no member state would 'need to pay more or receive less over the remainder of the current budget plan'.[13] Initially, the sum offered fell far short of the EU's demand. At the conclusion of phase 1 of the negotiations, however, the Joint Report of 8 December 2017 contained all financial obligations identified by the EU, including any future liabilities incurred before the end of 2020.[14]

Moreover, in her Florence speech, May requested a two-year transition period. The agreement reached in March 2018 followed the principled EU position that the UK would have all the legal rights and obligations of a member state, except for participation in decision-making, during transition. The UK also accepted the limited length of the transition period (until the end of 2020).[15]

The UK furthermore guaranteed the rights of EU citizens in the UK after withdrawal, including those that would move to the UK during the transition period. In an area of more genuine compromise, the UK agreed to incorporate the withdrawal agreement into UK law and to give the CJEU a formal role in the adjudication of the rights of EU citizens. This formal role was, however, limited to a period of eight years.[16]

Finally, the Irish border question has proven the thorniest issue in the negotiations. As the most affected member state, Ireland threatened to veto any agreement with the UK that would result in a hard border. In order to obtain a transition period and to start negotiations on the future relationship with the EU, the UK pledged to 'maintain full alignment with the rules of the Internal Market and the Customs Union' as a backstop solution.[17]

Halfway through the withdrawal process, the expected learning process has resulted in the increasing readiness of the UK government to make concessions, but not in a change of its preference for 'hard Brexit'. In a parallel development, clear majorities in public opinion expect economic losses and negative policy effects for the UK and understand that the EU has the upper hand in negotiations. Yet only a small majority has been thinking, since the summer of 2017, that the Brexit vote was a mistake, and there is no majority for stopping Brexit.[18]

Conclusions

In this article, I have outlined the theoretical similarities and differences between differentiated integration and differentiated disintegration and the change in negotiation context and bargaining power the UK is facing after moving from a defender of the status quo to a demander of disintegration. I formulated three enabling factors of the demand for disintegration in line with postfunctionalism but hypothesized that due to weak institutional and bargaining power states seeking disintegration would moderate their demands and make concessions to the EU in the course of negotiations.

So far, the Brexit case corroborates these expectations. First, the UK demand for disintegration fits the three enabling conditions: unintended integration effects challenging national identity and self-determination, the rise of a Eurosceptic party, and the availability of referendums. Moreover, the Leave campaign and the motivations for the Leave vote were in line with postfunctionalist expectations. Second, the Brexit negotiations and their intermediate outcomes are in line with the UK's weak institutional and material bargaining position. In negotiating a new settlement within the EU, Cameron only obtained a consolidation of the UK's existing differentiated integration, and in the withdrawal negotiations since the summer of 2017, the UK has made a series of concessions. Yet, even though the government and public are realizing the negative effects of Brexit and the weak bargaining power of the UK, there has not been a decisive change in the demand for a 'hard Brexit'. This finding speaks for the persistence of the identity and self-determination concerns that motivated the Brexit vote.

It is instructive to look beyond Brexit for comparable cases. So far, Brexit has remained the only case of differentiated disintegration by a member state.

Outside the EU, however, Switzerland has recently gone through a process of external differentiated disintegration. Similar to the UK, a combination of high migration from the EU, a strong Eurosceptic party (the Swiss People's Party), and abundant direct democratic opportunities puts bilateralism, the Swiss form of differentiated European integration, under recurring pressure. In February 2014, Swiss voters narrowly adopted the Mass Immigration Initiative, which mandated the government to negotiate and implement restrictions to the free movement of labour, including immigration quota and positive discrimination of Swiss nationals, and to refuse any future free movement agreements with the EU. These demands contradicted Switzerland's obligations under the Agreement on the Free Movement of Persons of 1999.

Like the UK, Switzerland was in a disadvantageous material bargaining position vis-à-vis the EU. The EU is by far Switzerland's most important trading partner, and the freedom of movement is linked legally to Switzerland's access to the internal market. In response to Switzerland's refusal to extend the free movement of persons to Croatia, the EU cancelled Switzerland's association to the EU's research policies and put the negotiation of several additional sectoral agreements on hold. Most importantly, it plainly refused to negotiate restrictions to the freedom of movement. Seeing how rigidly the EU defended the integrity of the internal market, the Swiss government resigned itself to implementing a light preference for domestic workers that disregarded the major provisions of the popular initiative and remained within the legal boundaries of the bilateral treaties. At the end of the day, Switzerland's unfavourable bargaining position overrode popular demand for differentiated disintegration.

The analysis in this article suggests that the learning process in the UK will continue as the negotiations on differentiated disintegration progress. Even though it does not predict where the process will end, the expected direction is clear – towards more UK concessions and a 'softer' Brexit.

Notes

1. Office for National Statistics, available at http://visual.ons.gov.uk/uk-perspectives-2016-trade-with-the-eu-and-beyond/ (accessed 3 April 2018).
2. Migration Watch UK, 'Net Migration Statistics', available at https://www.migrationwatchuk.org/statistics-net-migration-statistics (accessed 3 April 2018).
3. 'A New Settlement for the United Kingdom in a Reformed European Union', available at https://www.gov.uk/government/uploads/system/uploads/attachment_data/file/475679/Donald_Tusk_letter.pdf (accessed 3 April 2018).
4. 'Theresa May outlines "hard Brexit"', *EUobserver*, 17 January 2017, available at https://euobserver.com/uk-referendum/1365639 (accessed 3 April 2018).
5. 'Prime Minister's letter to Donald Tusk triggering Article 50', available at https://www.gov.uk/government/publications/prime-ministers-letter-to-donald-tusk-triggering-article-50 (accessed 3 April 2018).
6. See Endnote 5.

7. 'Fifty-fifty nation', *The Economist*, 19 November 2016.
8. See Endnote 5.
9. 'UK to depart EU court and Euratom', *EUobserver*, 13 July 2017, available at https://euobserver.com/uk-referendum/138524 (accessed 3 April 2018).
10. See Endnote 5; 'Hammond threatens the EU with aggressive tax changes after Brexit', *The Guardian*, 15 January 2017, available at https://www.theguardian.com/politics/2017/jan/15/philip-hammond-suggests-uk-outside-single-market-could-become-tax-haven (accessed 3 April 2018).
11. 'Tusk: No deal on Brexit would hit UK hardest', *EUobserver*, 15 March 2017, available at https://euobserver.com/uk-referendum/137250 (accessed 3 April 2018).
12. 'UK agrees to EU conditions on Brexit talks', *EUobserver*, 19 June 2017, available at https://euobserver.com/uk-referendum/138280 (accessed 3 April 2018).
13. 'May seeks EU grace period', *EUobserver*, 23 September 2017, available at https://euobserver.com/uk-referendum/139119 (accessed 3 April 2018).
14. 'Joint report from the negotiators of the European Union and the United Kingdom Government on progress during phase 1 of negotiations', available at https://ec.europa.eu/commission/sites/beta-political/files/joint_report.pdf (accessed 3 April 2018).
15. '"Decisive step ahead" in Brexit ahead of EU summit', *EUobserver*, 19 March 2018, available at https://euobserver.com/uk-referendum/14137 (accessed 3 April 2018).
16. See Endnote 14.
17. See Endnote 14.
18. YouGov UK, 'Where Britain stands on Brexit one year out', available at https://yougov.co.uk/news/2018/03/29/where-britain-stands-brexit-one-year-out/ (accessed 3 April 2018).

Acknowledgements

For valuable comments on previous versions of the article, I thank the anonymous reviewers as well as discussants and audiences at the Universities of Amsterdam and Duisburg-Essen, the 2017 conference of ECSA Suisse and a seminar of the UACES Collaborative Research Network on 'Differentiated Integration after Brexit' in Kristiansand, November 2017.

Disclosure statement

No potential conflict of interest was reported by the authors.

ORCID

Frank Schimmelfennig 🆔 http://orcid.org/0000-0002-1638-1819

References

Armstrong, K. (2017) *Brexit Time. Leaving the EU – Why, How and When?* Cambridge: Cambridge University Press.

Bale, T. (2016) '"Banging on about Europe": how the Eurosceptics got their referendum', available at http://eprints.lse.ac.uk/73062/1/blogs.lse.ac.uk-Banging%20on%20about%20Europe%20how%20the%20Eurosceptics%20got%20their%20referendum.pdf (accessed 3 April 2018).

Beramendi, P. (2012) *The Political Geography of Inequality: Regions and Redistribution*, Cambridge: Cambridge University Press.

Börzel, T. (2005) 'Mind the gap! European integration between level and scope', *Journal of European Public Policy* 12(2): 217–36.

Carey, S. (2002) 'Undivided loyalties: is national identity an obstacle to European integration?' *European Union Politics* 3(4): 387–413.

Clarke, H., Goodwin, M. and Whiteley, P. (2017) *Brexit. Why Britain Voted to Leave the European Union*, Cambridge: Cambridge University Press.

Dennison, J. and Geddes, A. (2018) 'Brexit and the perils of "Europeanised" immigration', *Journal of European Public Policy*. doi:10.1080/13501763.2018.1467953.

European Council (2014) 'European Council 26/27 June 2014 – conclusions' (EUCO 79/14).

European Council (2016) 'European Council meeting (18 and 19 February 2016) – conclusions' (EUCO 1/16).

European Council (2017) 'Special meeting of the European Council (Art. 50) (29 April 2017) – guidelines' (EUCO XT 20004/17).

Genschel, P. and Jachtenfuchs, M. (2014) 'Introduction: beyond market regulation. Analysing the European integration of core state powers', in P. Genschel and M. Jachtenfuchs (eds), *Beyond the Regulatory Polity? The European Integration of Core State Powers*, Oxford: Oxford University Press, pp. 1–23.

Jensen, M. and Snaith, H. (2016) 'When politics prevails: the political economy of a Brexit', *Journal of European Public Policy* 23(9): 1302–10.

Hobolt, S. (2016) 'The Brexit vote: a divided nation, a divided continent', *Journal of European Public Policy* 23(9): 1259–77.

Hooghe, L. and Marks, G. (2005) 'Calculation, community and cues: public opinion on European integration', *European Union Politics* 6(4): 419–43.

Hooghe, L. and Marks, G. (2009) 'A postfunctionalist theory of European integration: from permissive consensus to constraining dissensus', *British Journal of Political Science* 39(1): 1–23.

Kölliker, A. (2006) *Flexibility and European Unification: The Logic of Differentiated Integration*, Lanham: Rowman and Littlefield.

Leuffen, D., Rittberger, B. and Schimmelfennig, F. (2013) *Differentiated Integration. Explaining Variation in the European Union*, Basingstoke: Palgrave.

Menon, A. and Salter, J. (2016) 'Brexit: initial reflections', *International Affairs* 92(6): 1297–1318.

Möller, A. and Oliver, T. (2014) 'Conclusions', in A. Möller and T. Oliver (eds), *The United Kingdom and the European Union: What Would a 'Brexit' Mean for the EU and Other States Around the World?* Berlin: German Council on Foreign Relations (DGAPanalyse 16), available at https://dgap.org/en/article/getFullPDF/25763.

Oliver, T. (ed.) (2015) 'Cameron's letter: European views on the UK's renegotiation', available at http://blogs.lse.ac.uk/europpblog/2015/11/10/camerons-letter-european-views-on-the-uks-renegotiation/ (accessed 3 April 2018).

Oliver, T. (2016) 'European and international views of Brexit', *Journal of European Public Policy* 23(9): 1321–28.

Schimmelfennig, F. (2016) 'Good governance and differentiated integration. Graded membership in the European Union', *European Journal of Political Research* 55(4): 789–810.

Schimmelfennig, F. and Winzen, T. (2014) 'Instrumental and constitutional differentiation in the European Union', *JCMS: Journal of Common Market Studies* 52(2): 354–70.

Vollaard, H. (2014) 'Explaining European disintegration', *JCMS: Journal of Common Market Studies* 52(5): 1142–59.

Webber, D. (2014) 'How likely is it that the European Union will disintegrate? A critical analysis of competing theoretical perspectives', *European Journal of International Relations* 20(2): 341–65.

Weiss, S. and Blockmans, S. (2016) 'The EU deal to avoid Brexit: take it or leave', *CEPS Special Report 131*, Brussels: Centre for European Policy Studies.

Wennings, B. and Vines, E. (2016) 'Populism and sovereignty: the EU act and the in-out referendum, 2010–2015', *Parliamentary Affairs* 69(2): 309–26.

Winzen, T. and Schimmelfennig, F. (2016) 'Explaining differentiation in European Union treaties', *European Union Politics* 17(4): 616–37.

Back to the future? Franco-German bilateralism in Europe's post-Brexit union

Ulrich Krotz and Joachim Schild ⓘ

ABSTRACT
What are the consequences and implications of Brexit on the nature and character of Franco-German 'embedded bilateralism' in Europe, the relative influence of Berlin and Paris in EU policymaking, and the EU's future trajectory more generally? Brexit brings into sharper relief three basic future scenarios for the EU: (1) German hegemony; (2) the decline of the European project; and (3) a rejuvenated Franco-German tandem at the union's centre – what we call 'back to the future'. Which of these scenarios prevails will depend on the interaction of Brexit with other developments, most notably (1) the overall strengthening of Germany's relative standing, and (2) France's ability to overcome its economic and societal stasis with serious reforms. Though each of the three scenarios is possible, this paper holds that 'back to the future' is the most likely and plausible. Brexit thus might even further accentuate the historically influential Franco-German relationship, not least in union-level policy domains, such as security and defense, in which Britain has hitherto played a significant role.

Introduction

What are the main consequences and implications of Brexit on the nature and character of Franco-German 'embedded bilateralism' in Europe, the relative influence of Berlin and Paris in EU policymaking, and the EU's future trajectory more generally? Brexit brings into sharper relief three basic future scenarios for the EU: (1) German hegemony; (2) the degeneration, decline, or disintegration of the European project; and (3) the 'back to the future' possibility of a rejuvenated Franco-German link at the union's centre. Brexit alone, however, does not and cannot define or generate any of the three scenarios. Its impact will materialize in association with the unfolding of other developments, most notably (1) the overall strengthening of Germany's relative standing and the (open) question of which role Germany ultimately chooses to take on, most notably the slide into some sort of regional hegemony; and (2) France's ability (or inability) to overcome its economic and societal stasis with serious reforms to reenergize its economy. Together with these and other forces stemming from individual policy areas, Brexit, in principle, may influence the emergence of each possible scenario. Section One sketches the main features of these three trajectories-as-scenarios, considering the key factors that would either promote or hinder their appearance.

In conjunction with multiple underlying shifts and contingencies, the United Kingdom's exit will affect the dynamics of different policy areas in different ways. These changes across policy domains will, in turn, affect the EU's overall evolution. Brexit alters the actor constellations and preference configuration around the Brussels negotiating table. These changes affect the strategic options and potential coalition patterns among the member states – including the likelihood that French or German preferences will prevail in different EU policy fields – as well as the options for joint Franco-German initiatives and policy brokerage. Section Two briefly considers Brexit's implications for France, Germany, and France–Germany across the main policy domains in political economy; in foreign, security, and defence affairs; and on the possibilities for the flexible or differentiated integration of the EU's evolving polity (see also Schimmelfennig 2018).

In terms of Brexit's impact, we find no uniform logic across political domains, and no clear post-Brexit 'winner' in policy terms. But there is asymmetry. France, with its traditional policy orientations, clearly benefits more than Germany does in terms of its options and potential to shape EU policies. This rebalancing of influence in favour of France would dampen shifts toward radically more asymmetrical relations between France and Germany, curbing the likelihood of German hegemony in the post-Brexit EU. This would provide a favourable context for maintaining or even strengthening the Franco-German bilateral link and for joint European leadership.

This contribution advances two broad claims. First, Brexit alone neither defines the range of different futures for the EU (beyond its own exit), nor decisively determines any of the extant possible trajectories. Rather, Brexit is one among other causal factors that will combine with ongoing underlying shifts and developments that predate the 2016 Brexit vote. These include, most importantly, Germany's overall strengthening and increasingly prominent part in European affairs, and France's comparative economic malaise over the past decade.[1]

However, whether or not Germany eventually assumes a qualitatively different role on the continent and the union – ranging from markedly more determined leadership to some kind of 'regional hegemony' – will play out predominantly in the sphere of domestic politics and relates little and at best indirectly to Britain's 'exit'. The same diagnosis applies to the question of France's ability to halt or reverse its relative decline. The exact impact of Britain's EU exit on the roles and relative standings of France, Germany, and Franco-German embedded bilateralism in Europe, and thus on the EU's future, will depend on how these Brexit-unrelated forces further evolve and on how Brexit's effects intermingle with them. Thus, Brexit will take on its true causal weight, meaning, and direction.

Second, among the three basic future EU trajectories that Brexit helps to sharpen, the 'back to the future' of Franco-German embedded bilateralism emerges as the most likely and plausible scenario. Brexit, thus, might even further accentuate the importance of the historically influential Franco-German relationship, not least in policy domains in which Britain has hitherto played a significant role.

This is likely to be true for foreign, security, and defence policy, where Franco-German bilateralism could become decisive for Europe's future and its overall role and place in the world. Germany's (gradually) growing willingness to assume more responsibility in international politics, including an increased commitment to security and defence, further enhances this tendency. A stronger Germany and a yet more prominent EU role for France–Germany are not mutually exclusive; rather, they may complement and reinforce each other. The EU's internal policy domains are also likely to see France-Germany once again moving to centre stage, not least due to President Macron's attempt to revitalize French European policy by launching serious domestic reforms, as well as his strategic choice in favour of a reinvigorated Franco-German link as the best available option to promote French interests inside the EU (Schild 2017).

In stark contrast to the highly adverse impact of the British membership issue on Franco-German relations and European integration dynamics in the 1960s (following de Gaulle's double veto against British bids for entry), the Brexit vote has the potential to contribute to a relaunch of Franco-German bilateralism and a renewal of its contribution to European integration. Still, the other two scenarios – German hegemony or the European project's decline-degeneration-disintegration – remain realistic possibilities, especially if France fails to reform. This would give Brexit an altogether different causal spin and direction.

Trajectories as scenarios

With respect to France, Germany, and France-Germany in Europe, three basic scenarios have taken on clearer contours. Scenarios clarify what might be. They sharpen the main features of possible realities. They are not predictions, and they do not forecast single events or specific occurrences. Rather, they are exercises that help to structure our thinking and evaluate the probabilities of what will happen in the future.[2]

German hegemony

In this scenario, Brexit enhances a partially united Europe in some way dominated by a powerful Germany as its core state. 'Brexit would,' as the Economist (2016) puts it, 'upset[s] the balance of power, leaving more naked both German hegemony and French weakness'. Brexit further accentuates Germany's weight, influence, economic prowess, and geographic centrality, although not necessarily equally across all policy domains but presumably not strictly limited to economic and monetary affairs.[3]

Through Brexit, France and others certainly lose an ally to softly balance a stronger Germany within the EU, and to curb German influence. The tendency toward German prominence is further enhanced by its growing willingness to assume more responsibility in international politics, including in security and defence. On the other hand, through Brexit, Germany loses a market-oriented fellow member state to balance against those more sharply inclined toward protectionism and economic interventionism, frequently including France. Furthermore, as of now, Germany and the Germans continue to shy away from assuming the burdens, costs, risks, and responsibilities that regional hegemony would imply. Many among the elites, and most of the population, seem little prepared to take on the full role of a sharp(er)-edged international actor in a turbulent region and world. Often still inward-looking and self-centred, in what some view as its lingering passivity and moralism, Germany's overall leadership and its appetite to foot the bill for the provision of public European goods remains limited.

Though German strength and standing look to increase, for the foreseeable future, Germany will remain at best a 'reluctant hegemon' (Bulmer and Paterson 2013; Paterson 2011). Nonetheless, attitudes are subject to change, sometimes at a remarkable pace. As long as France is unsuccessful in reversing its relative decline, German regional hegemony remains a possibility on or just beyond the horizon.

Degeneration, decline, or disintegration of the European project

Brexit is a symptom and expression as well as a factor of the recent disintegrative dynamics, centrifugal forces, and degenerative tendencies of Europe's union. Post-Brexit, this scenario would entail further bouts of stalling or selective disintegration, presumably unevenly across policy domains, and significant spells of renationalization. It might involve prolonged periods of European 'muddling through' and the chronic bending or breaching of EU law or union-level agreements. It presumably would include further loss of popularity, respect, or legitimacy for the EU; further exits or loosening of member state commitments to the union; as well as a weakening, incapacitation, or break of the special bilateral Franco-German node that has characterized Europe over the past half-century. Ultimately, this scenario might usher in chronic degeneration or partial disintegration or, over time, evolve toward a 'more German' and perhaps eventually some sort of soft or uninspired regional hegemony.[4]

The table for this scenario is set. Brexit further fuels not just one EU-crisis, but a 'polycrisis' (Juncker): the confluence of myriad distinct crises feeding into each other. The current eurozone crisis is a sovereign debt crisis as well as a competitiveness one affecting many of Europe's economies. It also is a crisis of governance and institutional design. The European malaise is compounded by distrust of all political stripes in the institutions and machinery of Brussels. Today, no unifying purpose or vision convinces, unites, or inspires Europeans to support the European project in ways comparable to the enthusiasm generated by the ideal of 'no more war' following World War II.

Brexit would exemplify and fuel the EU-degeneration-decline scenario, but it is hardly its key cause. In addition to the leadership role that Germany might (or might not) assume, France's inability to restore its international competitiveness, fix its broken social model, and overcome its political and societal stasis would be this scenario's root cause. Yet, Emmanuel Macron has a very clear mandate to rebuild France. His first year in office showed his resolve to implement sweeping economic and welfare state reforms. The successful implementation of his contentious labour market reform in September 2017 testifies to this determination.

Working through the close links with Germany to consolidate and renew the European project is a basic strategic pillar of his presidency. To date, Macron and all German interlocutors clearly work against the disintegration-degeneration-decline trajectory. If President Macron fails, however, and if Germany proves unwilling or unable to step in to provide stronger leadership and EU-wide public goods, this type of future, in one form or another, will become more likely.

Embedded bilateralism: back to the future

According to a recent EU-wide survey among policy-makers and experts, other member states consider Germany and France (in that order) to be their 'essential partners' in European policy-making. Moreover, Germany and France each consider the other as their essential partner. In various policy fields from foreign policy, security and defence to economic, social and fiscal policy, the two constitute the inner circle of EU coalition-building (Janning and Zunneberg 2017: 7–8). Surveys conducted among Council working groups to uncover network structures and using a large dataset on legislative decision-making (Huhe et al. 2017) conclude that Brexit will further strengthen France's and Germany's central network positions. Some expect 'decision outcomes with more regulation and higher subsidies in a post-Brexit EU', which would be closer to French rather than German preferences (Huhe et al. 2017: 3).

In this scenario, France and Germany and a reenergized bilateralism will uphold and reform a firmer and more credible EU in times of European turmoil and strong internal and external challenges. France and Germany together will act as a force of cohesion, preserving the union's integrated core, both geographically and functionally, from the single market to the Schengen free travel area and the eurozone, and, presumably, increasingly in foreign policy, security, and defence. A recharged embedded bilateralism could mean not just tinkering with the symptoms of the crises, but wielding sustainable consolidation of solutions that take 'EU' beyond its seeming association with crisis, calamity, or dissatisfaction. This will probably comprise winning back support for the European project and, perhaps, a sense of purpose across most member states' elites and populations.

In some ways, this scenario may be reminiscent of the EC prior to UK accession. Yet, it would carry a distinct twenty-first century appearance. It would probably see a stronger and more active Germany than, say, at the times of Adenauer–de Gaulle, Schmidt–Giscard, or even Kohl–Mitterrand. However, more German leadership, not least in foreign relations, security, and defence, does not rule out a more prominent role for France-Germany within Europe, and is something altogether different from German hegemony (as already illustrated by its dealings with Russia in the wake of the Crimea annexation and Ukraine crisis; see Krotz and Maher 2016: 1057–1061).

A functional Franco-German embedded bilateralism, as in the past, is likely to be a necessary condition for problem-solving or consolidation at the Union level but hardly a sufficient one in an ever more heterogeneous EU-27. This scenario is not necessarily idyllic or happy for all. In fact, it is exactly what the Visegrád countries (Czech Republic, Hungary, Poland and Slovakia) fear. They perceive the United Kingdom as a countervailing force against the dominant role of Germany and France – as the Benelux countries did in the 1960s (and to a certain extent still today). Further, the Visegrád group countries fear a deeper integration around the eurozone or an attempt to build a core Europe that excludes them in a post-Brexit EU (Lang 2016: 1). The more assertive and exclusive the Franco-German leadership ambition, the more resistance it is likely to meet among the other 25 members.

The key precondition for this scenario is France's ability to reform its economy, political system, or polity as a whole. A modernized and rejuvenated France could provide a solid basis for a renewed bilateral link and viable embedded bilateralism. If Macron only partially succeeds in enacting reforms at home, a Franco-German 'back to the future' embedded bilateralism, albeit adjusted to twenty-first century realities, is a plausible trajectory. Otherwise, the future will more likely tilt toward the two other scenarios.

Political domains and policy dynamics

With Brexit, the union loses a state that has supported market liberalism; the deepening of the single market, especially in financial services; open international trade; economic and cultural globalization; and the subsidiary principle. Britain has also been an important net contributor to the budget. In reverse, it has been sceptical towards increasing EU centralization, about Eurocrats' and French pleas for more union-level harmonization in social affairs or taxation, and hostile to a hollowing out of NATO's role in Europe. Besides France, it has been the only member with a truly global outlook in foreign and security affairs. It has reacted allergically to high-flying European dreams and ill-founded promises but defended a very pragmatic, sober, and results-oriented approach to European affairs (George 1998). Does Brexit strengthen either France or Germany in EU policy-making in given political domains, such that it tilts the balance of influence and power in favour of one of the two and/or alters their bilateral relationship? Did the United Kingdom block integration in certain policy fields advocated by France and or Germany? Will Brexit thus facilitate new options?

Political economy areas – single market, international trade, union budget, Eurozone governance

Without the United Kingdom, Germany (and other market-oriented member states such as Ireland, Sweden, and the Netherlands) will lose an ally in single market issues against those more sharply inclined towards economic interventionism, supportive of an active industrial policy, and reluctant to endorse a liberalization agenda (Kroll and Leuffen 2016: 1314; Oliver 2016: 1323). The 'market shaping' coalition on single market issues will be strengthened at the expense of a hitherto UK-led 'market making' coalition (Quaglia 2010). France might take advantage of Brexit when following its deeply-ingrained *dirigiste* and at times protectionist instincts and its harmonization agenda in social and economic policies.

Germany, however, does not consistently occupy the liberal end of a market liberalization vs. regulation continuum. Germany, together with France, was part of the market-shaping rather than the UK-led market-making advocacy coalition on financial market liberalization/regulation issues (Quaglia 2010: 1010).[5] With Brexit, the EU loses a fervent advocate, the 'pace-setter' (and main beneficiary) of the most important current project on single market liberalization: the Capital Market Union (CMU) (Howarth and Quaglia 2017: 152). Both Germany and France lent much more cautious support to this Commission initiative, backed mainly by the United Kingdom, Ireland, Sweden, the Netherlands, and Luxembourg. Paris and Berlin expressed reservations regarding the merits of a US-style capital market-based system of business financing sources (Quaglia et al. 2016: 198–199). Brexit will strengthen their position in future negotiations on CMU legislation.

On issues of international free trade, Germany loses an ally against French protectionist temptations. France has long advocated new and stronger protectionist instruments in the framework of the EU's autonomous trade policy against unfair trade practices. Paris promotes the principle of reciprocity in market access and it calls for stronger control of foreign direct investment in strategic economic sectors. On the latter point, Germany's willingness to follow France has grown as a consequence of the Chinese Midea Group's successful takeover of Kuka, the leading German high-tech robotics manufacturer, in 2016. Recently, Germany has subscribed more broadly to the French trade policy agenda. The two governments together have advocated reinforcement of the EU's defensive trade policy instruments, promoted the idea of more reciprocity in market access in public procurement, and asked the Commission, together with Italy, to work on a proposal allowing member states to better protect their strategic industries against third country FDIs (Conseil des Ministres Franco-Allemand 2017). The odds of getting their way are rising with Brexit.

These German adjustments notwithstanding, the trade policy outlook of export champion Germany will, for structural reasons, remain more liberal-minded than the preferences of France and the Mediterranean countries, which are plagued by international competitiveness problems and, compared to Germany, have a lower share of extra-EU exports relative to overall exports. Brexit will tilt the balance of power inside the EU towards this group of countries. It is not a coincidence that French president Macron is much more sceptical and cautious than is the German government regarding market opening in the framework of trade agreements under negotiation with Mercosur, Japan, Australia, and New Zealand.

Brexit's impact on French and German contributions to the EU's budget will also be asymmetrical. Germany and France are the two most important net contributors to the budget in absolute terms, the United Kingdom ranking third (Haas and Rubio 2017). But unlike Germany, France does not have its own 'rebate' when it comes to financing the UK's rebate (Germany, along with Austria, the Netherlands, and Sweden, pay only 25% of their normal share of the UK abatement). Germany signalled its willingness to contribute more than it has in the past – and more in relation to France – to plug holes in the EU budget caused by the British exit (Coalition Treaty 2018). The balance of power in budgetary politics will shift in favour of the net recipients. But Germany is likely to lose its pivotal position in future negotiations on the EU's Multiannual Financial Framework between the hard stance of the United Kingdom and the demands of net recipients (Becker 2017: 12). As a member state with lower net contributions, in the future France might find itself in a key position to advance compromises between the opposing camps of net contributors and net recipients.

Brexit will profoundly affect the relationship between the euro-ins and euro-outs. The latter fear a second-class status following a deeper integration and separate institutions for the eurozone; they will lose a key coalition partner. The euro-outs will have a harder time resisting the euro-ins' attempts to deepen the institutional, legal, and political lines dividing them in a multi-speed Europe. Therefore, Brexit contributes to opening a reform window in eurozone governance. On the one hand, this creates an opportunity for a revival of Franco-German bilateralism, as both are committed to eurozone governance reforms. This debate gathered momentum with the election of Emmanuel Macron in France and the reform proposals he put forward during his election campaign: a eurozone budget, a European minister of finance, and a eurozone parliament. On the other hand, the combined effects of Brexit and the French election put pressure on Germany to accept more financial redistribution and risk-sharing. The German government's coalition treaty testifies to its willingness to 'strengthen the principle of mutual solidarity' (Coalition Treaty 2018: 6).

The electoral strength of the right-wing populist Alternative für Deutschland (AfD), however, constrains the new government's room for compromise. These domestic constraints might strengthen the German call for transforming the European Stability Mechanism (ESM) into a European Monetary Fund with powers to enforce fiscal rules. But it is unlikely to garner French support without also introducing some elements of risk sharing. However, the more Germany closes ranks with France on euro area risk-sharing issues, the more it undermines support from Northern member states for any Franco-German leadership role on EMU reform. In a recent so-called 'non-paper' eight Northern member states signalled their limited willingness to follow a Franco-German lead based on 'far-reaching proposals', stressed the need of risk reduction and called for discussions in an 'inclusive format' (Northern Eight Non-paper 2018).

Brexit changes the actor constellations and hence the potential coalitions in the EU. According to Sinn (2017), it will lead to major power shifts in the Council. A German-led coalition of like-minded member states favouring free trade and a liberal economic order – including Austria, the Netherlands, Finland, and (so far) the United Kingdom – will see its population share shrink from 35 to only 26% after Brexit. Hence, it loses its blocking majority in QMV decision-making in the Council according to the 35% population criterion. The 'Club Med' states (France, Greece, Italy, Portugal, and Spain), on the contrary, will see their share of the EU population rise from 25% to 44% after Brexit.[6] France, Italy, and Spain alone move from 34% to 39% of the EU's population and thus need only one additional state as a coalition partner to build a blocking minority in the Council (requiring four member states with at least 35% of the EU's population). This 'Mediterranean triangle' is characterized by 'strong reciprocal ties among all actors' (Zunneberg 2017: 5). Furthermore, the voting behaviour of France, Italy, and Spain is much more consistent with each other than with Germany (Frantescu 2017). Whereas Germany has not consistently sided with the liberal pro-market liberalization coalition – comprising the United Kingdom, Ireland, the Scandinavian countries, and several Eastern European countries – it often had a pivotal role and could tilt the balance towards either the market-making or the market-shaping coalition (Göllner 2017). This might change after Brexit, as the relative institutional power resources of France, Italy, and Spain increase.

Foreign policy, security, and defence

Shorter-term factors, and longer-term shifts, are likely to boost the signifi-cance and impact of Franco-German bilateralism and EU commitment in the domains of foreign policy, security, and defence. Brexit is just one among other factors and forces likely to enhance these trends. It will thus con-tribute to boosting not only the role of France and Germany but, ironically and counter-intuitively perhaps, will also significantly strengthen European inte-gration in areas where it traditionally has often proceeded only slowly and with difficulty.[7] Brexit coincides with a period in which defence spending in Europe has begun to rise again, and Germany's reluctance to more seriously engage regionally and internationally, specifically in security and defence, is (slowly) waning. These factors will not immediately fully offset Britain's exit, but they will help to smooth the transition.

More generally, the EU's dramatically changing international environment and increasing external pressures, equally profound and evolving, provide strong incentives for France and Germany and the EU as a whole to intensify their security and defence efforts as well as their search for greater strategic autonomy for Europe. To its east, an assertive and resurgent Russia, not least through its Crimea annexation and proxy war in eastern Ukraine, has brought geopolitics back to the continent. To its south and southeast, the arc of instability – with its recurrent violence in the Mideast and the unsettled post-Arab 'spring' Maghreb – will not disappear anytime soon. And to its west, the strategic reorientation of the United States toward East Asia and the Pacific, ongoing with or without a President Trump, is likely to have longer-term implications that will prompt or force the Europeans, including the Germans, to commit more seriously to taking care of their own security and defence. As Chancellor Merkel put it during a speech in Munich in May 2017: 'the time when we could entirely rely on others is somewhat over (…) We Europeans must really take our fate into our own hands' (Spiegel online 2017) – a statement that might herald a paradigm shift in German foreign and security policy (Hellmann 2017).

While causing troubles in the short term, Brexit is unlikely to undermine the EU's Common Security and Defence Policy (CSDP). Britain has ranked only fifth among EU member states in troop contributions to CSDP military operations, and seventh in civilian CSDP personnel contributions (Faleg 2016). In some respects, it has hindered CSDP's development, for example, by slowing or impeding greater integration in security and defence, and by frequently prioritizing NATO. In specific instances, the United Kingdom blocked efforts to establish a permanent operational military headquarter for the EU and opposed CSDP intervention in the Democratic Republic of Congo in 2008 (The Guardian 2008; The Telegraph 2011). In addition, London opposed both an institutional strengthening of the European Defence Agency and an increase in its budget.

Still, France loses the only EU partner sharing its global strategic outlook in foreign and security affairs, and its readiness to use military means to promote its interests and values on the international scene. Paris could compensate for this loss by developing closer bilateral links with the post-Brexit United Kingdom in line with the bilateral approach adopted by the two during the last decade, when they signed the Lancaster House treaty in 2010 on defence, security, and nuclear co-operation. Indeed, French President Macron made the case for 'a strong and pragmatic relationship with a post-Brexit Britain, working together on defence and counter-terrorism because of the two countries' "linked destinies"' (The Guardian 2017). A renewed intensity of Franco-British relations in this policy field would be all the more likely if attempts to revitalize and develop the EU's foreign, security, and defence policy come to nothing and if Germany proves unwilling to take a more active and less risk-averse role in international politics.

As of now, however, it does not appear likely that France will have to turn to the United Kingdom due to a German lack of interest in developing European security and defence co-operation. Among the policy fields in which Germany and France might be able to infuse a new dynamic into EU-level co-operation, security and defence policy stands out. During and after Brexit, the United Kingdom will lose its ability to hamper or block initiatives strengthening the EU's military capacities, decision-making structures, and ambitions.

The empirical evidence available so far, a slew of initiatives, policy projects, and stated intentions certainly document that Franco-German co-operation in the areas of foreign policy, security, and defence is gathering momentum. Already, four days after the Brexit referendum, a declaration of the two foreign ministers suggested making use – for the first time ever – of the Lisbon Treaty's clause on permanent structured co-operation (Articles 42[6] and 46 of the Treaty on European Union-TEU) in military matters (Ayrault and Steinmeier 2016). It allows for the creation of a subgroup of Member States committing themselves to strict criteria with regard to the development of their defence capacities as well as their participation in European equipment programmes and multinational forces.

In September 2016, the two defence ministers, Le Drian and von der Leyen, followed up by tabling a substantial common contribution, laying out a roadmap towards a revitalized CSDP. Besides calling for permanent structured co-operations (PESCOs), they advocated – among other ideas – a permanent EU military and civilian planning and conduct capability, regular European Council meetings on security and defence issues, common financing of CSDP missions, and the establishment of strategic European transport capacities and a European Medical Command (Le Drian and von der Leyen 2016).

Perhaps most remarkably, at the 19th Franco-German Ministerial Council of July 2017, the two countries announced the launch of a European initiative in favour of a PESCO, defining a common approach to the criteria allowing partner countries to participate. This initiative quickly gathered speed as the Foreign and Defence Ministers from 23 Member States agreed on launching a PESCO on 13 November 2017, a step endorsed by the European Council in December (European Council 2017: 1). This will provide a test case in how far the German insistence on inclusiveness of subgroups on defence issues will limit the level of ambition.

Furthermore, in the field of armament and procurement, France and Germany envisage the development and procurement of the next generation's major weapon systems: tanks, artillery systems, combat aircraft, and combat helicopters. A common project developing drones together with Italy is already underway, and a high-level Franco-German working group focuses on concrete proposals in this field (Conseil des Ministres Franco-Allemand 2017). The dynamics of Franco-German security and defence cooperation and France's willingness of to invest in the CSDP framework will, however, crucially depend on Germany's readiness to increase defence spending and take part in military interventions, and hence to share costs and risks. Wide segments of Germany's political leadership and the general public continue to resist a more active security and especially defence role for their country. Nevertheless, there is 'currently a real window of opportunity for Paris and Berlin to take European defence cooperation to the next level' (Kempin and Kunz 2017: 28).

European polity and institutional frame

Brexit reveals fundamental differences among member states as to the underlying social purpose of European integration. Accordingly, the foreign ministers of France and Germany made the case for finding 'better ways to deal with different levels of ambition' in the EU, particularly hinting at defence, asylum, migration, and eurozone governance as policy areas in which subgroups might move ahead (Ayrault and Steinmeier 2016). At the bilateral Franco-German Ministerial Council in July 2017, the two states spelled out their ideas on increased subgroup co-ordination, especially in the domain of defence (Conseil des Ministres Franco-Allemand 2017).

The United Kingdom's EU withdrawal removes a very high obstacle on the road towards such an enhanced subgroup co-operation in key policy fields. Strongly pushed by France and with more German support than ever before, this idea was taken up by the Benelux countries in their common 'Vision on the Future of Europe' (Michel 2017) and made its way into the Rome declaration, on the occasion of the EEC's 60th anniversary (25 March 2017), underlining the intention to 'act together, at different paces and intensity where necessary'. Even the Commission – traditionally hostile to schemes of flexible integration – in its March 2017 White Paper depicted it as one of several imaginable trajectories on the future of Europe. This option found support in France, Germany, Spain, and Italy (Chang 2017: 13).

In the past, France and Germany had initiated all major steps of flexible integration and deepening of integration in subgroups – the European Monetary System and later Union, the Schengen Agreement, the Fiscal Compact – with the notable exception of the Banking Union (Schild 2018). Brexit is likely to reenergize Paris and Berlin's lead in moving the EU toward ever more flexible integration schemes, and 'variable geometry' is likely to regain importance with Brexit. Providing the inner ring of the EU's political centre, 'France and Germany are very likely to emerge at the core of any future initiative' to deepen cooperation in subgroups of member states (Janning and Zunneberg 2017: 13). Table 1 summarizes this section's findings and considerations.

Table 1. The impact of Brexit: shifting influence of France and Germany in different fields.

	Germany	France
single market	weakened where Germany advocates liberalization, strengthened where Germany is part of a market shaping coalition	France strengthened as key player in market shaping coalitions
trade	overall weakened; but partially strengthened where Germany seeks protectionist instruments	strengthened, key demands in terms of protectionist instruments meet with less resistance
union budget	weakened, demands for higher German contributions, less pivotal role in MFF negotiations	strengthened, potential pivotal role in MFF negotiations
eurozone governance	strengthened when supporting eurozone reform agenda, but increasing demands for German fiscal transfers	strengthened, fewer obstacles on the road to ambitious reform
foreign policy and defence	strengthened, more ambitious international role, common Franco-German leadership in promoting permanent structured cooperation in defence	strengthened, common Franco-German leadership in promoting permanent structured cooperation in defence
polity	strengthened, common leadership role with France in promoting key integration projects in subgroups	strengthened, common leadership role with Germany in promoting key integration projects in subgroups

Conclusions

Brexit is an important marker in the history and politics of the European project, with potentially significant implications for Franco-German 'embedded bilateralism' in Europe as well as the two countries' individual roles, standings, and influence within the bilateral link and with the EU at large. It will markedly affect the policy dynamics across key EU political domains. Yet, by itself, it does not (re-)define the range of the EU's possible future trajectories, nor the roles of France, Germany, or France–Germany in them. Rather, in its impact on the EU's overall future trajectory, Brexit will combine with other forces and factors, functioning as a catalyst for some trends while accelerating, enhancing, or obstructing other shifts and tendencies.

Whether the EU drifts toward German hegemony, disintegration-degeneration-decline, or a 'back-to-the future' of Franco-German embedded bilateralism will importantly depend on the extent to which Germany takes on more leadership; the risks and burdens of stronger engagement for the union as a whole across policy domains, but especially in security and defence; and France's ability to pursue domestic reforms, revitalizing its economy, society, and political system, and reversing its decline inside the EU. Evolutions, developments, ruptures, or breakdowns of any of these will give Brexit's implications a particular spin or direction. Brexit is an ingredient of a larger (and more complex) European brew.

Brexit's effects on the policy dynamics across the main political EU domains do not generate a clear 'winner' (or 'loser'). But there is an asymmetry that benefits France rather than Germany and that, overall, favours France's potential to shape EU policies in accordance with traditional French orientations. In addition, the United Kingdom's future absence in the Council will provide yet more opportunity, weight, and potential to joint Franco-German initiatives and European co-leadership.

This is certainly true for the areas of foreign, security, and defence policy where, thanks to its experience, military assets, and professional diplomacy, Britain was a key union player. In these domains, Britain's exit removes significant hindrances to greater union-ambitions and engagement, from institution-building (for example the creation of union-military headquarters and the strengthening of the European Defence Agency) or deeper integration toward joint forces, assets, arms procurement, and defence industries, among others. These areas are highly likely to experience new bouts of integration, and the Franco-German node a more prominent role than it has seen before.[8]

In the key political economy domains, Brexit favours French interests, preferences, and options for coalitions and brinkmanship in the Council. This Brexit-induced causal twist might at least partially offset the overall rise of

Germany's standing and influence – a meaningful shift on the continent over the past decade-and-a-half. No matter exactly how much Brexit favours France in policy fields such as single market matters, international trade, union budget, or eurozone governance, a stronger Germany and an even more prominent role for Franco-German embedded bilateralism in Europe are hardly mutually exclusive, but rather complement and reinforce each other. In fact, Brexit might actually fuel a new mix or phase of the Franco-German node.

Britain's union exodus is also highly likely to remove obstacles to greater emphasis on differentiated forms and speeds of integration. Again, Brexit does not cause, but simplifies and accelerates the trend towards a multi-speed Europe or permanent forms of variable geometry as a suitable way for the EU to accommodate the heterogeneity of its member states and their differing ideas on the purpose of the EU. The growing 'demand' for differentiated subgroup co-operation with its intergovernmentalism (as in the prior history of European integration) provides ample opportunities for Franco-German agenda-setting, policy initiatives, and compromise-building around core post-Brexit projects.

So far, we can observe a strong resolve in Paris and Berlin to take up the challenge of Brexit and the wider 'polycrisis' and to seize the opportunities that come with them in terms of a renewal of their joint influence and leadership on key projects. After the French elections, Merkel and Macron made a clear and deliberate choice in favour of renewing and reenergizing older patterns of Franco-German bilateralism and its nodal position in the European project.

Table 2 summarizes the preceding sections' considerations. In case of various contingencies, the cells highlight in bold the factor's most likely impact. (The table refrains from an assessment on the degree of success or failure of reforming France.) Taken together, these considerations and available evidence seem to support the likelihood of the 'back-to-the-future' of a renewed embedded bilateralism-scenario, rather than 'German hegemony' or disintegration-degeneration-decline.

Brexit has certainly sharpened French and German leaders' perceptions of the challenges confronting the European project, its possible futures, and France and Germany's common responsibility to prevent it from unravelling. Note, however, that crucial factors for a determined renewal of Franco-German embedded bilateralism are located at the domestic level with its own logics: Will the German public and political elites subscribe to the idea of Germany taking on more responsibility regionally and internationally – along with the associated risks and costs? Will the new French president Macron overcome the multiple obstacles on the road towards fixing France's broken economic and social model? Only time will tell. If Germany turns its back to the union (or decisively bids for real regional hegemony),

Table 2. Key factors and scenarios.

Scenario factor	German hegemony	disintegration	back to the future
greater German leadership, more engagement, and/or strong(er) commitment to provide European public goods	undermines, if absent or rejected; **neutral, if moderate;** favours, if very strong	**undermines, if moderate** or (very) strong; favours if rejected or reduced	undermines, if rejected or reduced; **strongly favours, if moderate;** neutral if (very) strong
extent and success of French domestic (economic) reforms	undermines if successful or very successful; permissive if failure	undermines if successful or very successful; favours if failure	undermines if failure; strongly favours if successful or very successful
change in Council preference configurations and coalition options across key policy fields, asymmetrically favouring France	**undermines**	**neutral**	**favours or strongly favours joint initiative and co-leadership**
differentiated integration, 'multi-speed,' 'variable geometry'	**neutral**	**undermines**	**favours or strongly favours**
deliberate choice in Paris and Berlin for renewed Franco-German bilateralism	**undermines**	**undermines**	**favours or strongly favours**

and/or if France fails to reform and modernize, the 'disintegration-degeneration-decline' or the 'German hegemony' scenarios are bound to forcefully re-enter the scene as realistic continental futures, giving Brexit a quite different casual direction and meaning.

Notes

1. Thus viewed, Brexit does not represent in and of itself a 'genetic moment' in Capoccia and Kelemen's (2007; quote from 342) take on path dependence.
2. For a methodological outline informing our employment of scenarios, including their relevance for policy, see, for example, Weber 1996.
3. The exact shape or form of German regional hegemony would be important – whether a Kindlebergerian model, stressing the burdens and responsibilities of leadership and regional public goods provision, or one with the harder edges of regional domination of an offensive realist sort. For different views (and types) of hegemony, see Clark 2011; Kindleberger 1973; Mearsheimer 2001. On German hegemony and its issues, note Bulmer and Paterson 2013; Paterson 2011; Schönberger 2012.
4. The best theoretically informed work on possible EU disintegration or decline to date includes Schimmelfennig 2018; Vollaard 2014; Webber 2014. For a debate on the sources and future prospects of European integration, see Krotz and Maher et al. 2012.
5. On the impact of Brexit on European financial market integration and regulation, see Howarth and Quaglia 2018.
6. Data from Eurostat (1 January 2016).
7. On France–Germany in these areas over the past half century and today, see Krotz and Schild 2013, chapter 9; Krotz and Wolf 2018. On the fitful rise of EU foreign and security policy from the perspective of general international

relations theory, see Krotz and Maher 2011; for consideration of specific political factors propelling or undermining the EU's emergence as a full political actor in international affairs, see Krotz 2009.
8. For a cautious assessment, see Deubner 2018.

Acknowledgments

This paper has benefited from presentations at the 113th Annual Meeting of the American Political Science Association (APSA) in San Francisco, 31 August-3 September 2017; the UACES 47th Annual Conference in Krakow, 4–6 September 2017; and the Institut für europäische Integrationsforschung at the University of Vienna. For comments on earlier versions of this article, we thank Thomas Angerer, Martin Bull, Erik Jones, Jonathan Joseph, Richard Maher, Monika Mühlböck, Claire Thirriot-Kwant, and three anonymous reviewers. For valuable editorial support, we thank Sarah Tarrow. The usual disclaimer applies.

Disclosure statement

No potential conflict of interest was reported by the authors.

ORCID

Joachim Schild ⓘ https://orcid.org/0000-0001-6149-8007

References

Ayrault, J.-M. and Steinmeier, F.-W. (2016) 'A strong Europe in a world of uncertainties', 25 June, available at https://www.auswaertiges-amt.de/EN/Europa/Aktuell/160624-BM-AM-FRA_ST.html (accessed 25 July 2017).
Becker, P. (2017) 'Der Brexit und die Folgen für den Europäischen Haushalt', Schriftliche Stellungnahme zur Öffentlichen Anhörung des Ausschusses für die Angelegenheiten der Europäischen Union des Deutschen Bundestages am 24 April 2017, Ausschussdrucksache 18(21) 101, 83. Sitzung.
Bulmer, S. and Paterson, W.E. (2013) 'Germany as the EU's reluctant hegemon? Of economic strength and political constraints', *Journal of European Public Policy* 20(10): 1387–405.
Capoccia, G. and Kelemen, R.D. (2007) 'The study of critical junctures: theory, narrative, and counterfactuals in historical institutionalism', *World Politics* 59(3): 341–69.

Chang, M. (2017) 'Brexit and EMU: from EMU outsider to instigator', *CSF-SSUP Working Paper Series, No 4*.

Clark, I. (2011) *Hegemony in International Society*, Oxford: Oxford University Press.

Coalition Treaty (2018) 'Ein neuer Aufbruch für Europa. Eine neue Dynamik für Deutschland. Ein neuer Zusammenhalt für unser Land', Koalitionsvertrag zwischen CDU, CSU und SPD, Berlin, 7 February 2018.

Conseil des Ministres Franco-Allemand / Deutsch-Französischer Ministerrat, Paris, 13.7.2017, documents available at http://www.elysee.fr/assets/Uploads/Conseil-des-ministres-franco-allemand2.pdf (accessed 23 July 2017).

Deubner, C. (2018) *Security and Defence Cooperation in the EU: A Matter of Utility and Choice*, Baden-Baden: Nomos.

Economist (2016) 'Brexit brief: How others see it', 30 April.

European Council (2017) 'Conclusions, European council meeting', Brussels, 14 December 2017 (EUCO 19/1/17).

Faleg, G. (2016) 'The implications of Brexit for the EU's common security and defence policy', CEPS, 26 July 2016, available at https://www.ceps.eu/publications/implications-brexit-eu%E2%80%99s-common-security-and-defence-policy#_ftn2 (accessed 24 July 2017).

Frantescu, D.P. (2017) 'France more likely than Germany to lead EU council after Brexit, voting records in the council show', VoteWatch Europe, 29 March, available at http://www.votewatch.eu/blog/france-more-likely-than-germany-to-lead-the-eu-council-after-brexit-voting-records-in-the-council-show/ (accessed 25 July 2017).

George, S. (1998) *An Awkward Partner: Britain in the European Community*, 3rd ed., Oxford: Oxford University Press.

Göllner, R.T. (2017) 'The Visegrád group – A rising star post-brexit? changing distribution of power in the european Council', *Open Political Science* 1: 1–6.

Haas, J. and Rubio, E. (2017) 'Brexit and the EU budget: threat or opportunity', Paris: Notre Europe/Institut Jacques Delors, Policy Paper 183, 16 January, available at http://www.institutdelors.eu/media/brexiteubudget-haasrubio-jdi-jan17.pdf?pdf=ok (accessed 7 March 2018).

Hellmann, G. (2017) 'Deutschland, die Europäer und ihr Schicksal. Herausforderungen deutscher Außenpolitik nach einer Zeitenwende', *Zeitschrift für Staats- und Europawissenschaften* 15(2–3): 329–46.

Howarth, D. and Quaglia, L. (2017) 'Brexit and the single European financial market', *JCMS: Journal of Common Market Studies* 55(Annual Review): 149–64.

Howarth, D. and Quaglia, L. (2018) 'Brexit and the battle for financial services', *Journal of European Public Policy* 25(8): 1118–36.

Huhe, N., Naurin, D. and Thomson, R. (2017) 'Legislative decision-making and network relations in the European Union after the United Kingdom leaves', Paper presented for the Annual Meeting of the American Political Science Association, San Francisco, 31 August 2017.

Janning, J. and Zunneberg, C. (2017) 'The invisible web: from interaction to coalition-building in the European Union', European Council of Foreign Relations, Policy Brief, May.

Kempin, R. and Kunz, B. (2017) *France, Germany, and the Quest for European Strategic Autonomy: Franco-German Defence Cooperation in A New Era*, Berlin and Paris: SWP and IFRI, Note du Cerfa, 141.

Kindleberger, C.P. (1973) *The World in Depression, 1929–1939*, Berkeley: University of California Press.

Kroll, D.A. and Leuffen, D. (2016) 'Ties that bind, can also strangle: the Brexit threat and the hardships of reforming the EU', *Journal of European Public Policy* 23(9): 1311–20.

Krotz, U. (2009) 'Momentum and impediments: why Europe won't emerge as a full political actor on the world stage soon', *JCMS: Journal of Common Market Studies* 47(3): 555–78.

Krotz, U. and Maher, R. (2011) 'International relations theory and the rise of European foreign and security policy', *World Politics* 63(3): 548–79.

Krotz, U. and Maher, R. (2016) 'Europe's crises and the EU's "big three"', *West European Politics* 39(5): 1053–72.

Krotz, U. and Schild, J. (2013) *Shaping Europe: France, Germany, and Embedded Bilateralism from the Elysée Treaty to Twenty-First Century Politics*, Oxford: Oxford University Press.

Krotz, U. and Wolf, K. (2018) 'Franco-German defence and security cooperation', in H. Meijer and M. Wyss (eds.), *The Handbook of European Defence Policies and Armed Forces*, Oxford: Oxford University Press, pp. 440–57.

Krotz, Ulrich and Richard Maher, David M. McCourt and Andrew Glencross, Norrin M. Ripsman, Mark S. Sheetz and Jean-Yves Haine, and Sebastian Rosato (2012) 'Debating the sources and prospects of European integration', *International Security* 37(1): 178–99.

Lang, K.-O. (2016) 'Die Visegrád-Staaten und der Brexit', Berlin: Stiftung Wissenschaft und Politik, *SWP aktuell* 53.

Le Drian, J.-Y. and von der Leyen, U. (2016) 'Revitalizing CSDP: towards a comprehensive, realistic and credible defence in the EU', Berlin, 12 September 2016, available at https://www.senato.it/japp/bgt/showdoc/17/DOSSIER/990802/3_propositions-franco-allemandes-sur-la-defense.pdf (accessed 13 August 2017).

Mearsheimer, J.J. (2001) *The Tragedy of Great Power Politics*, New York: Norton.

Michel, C. (2017) 'Benelux vision on the future of Europe', 3 February, available at http://premier.fgov.be/en/benelux-vision-future-europe (accessed 26 July 2017).

Northern Eight Non Paper 2018 'Finance ministers of Denmark, Estonia, Finland, Ireland, Latvia, Lithuania, the Netherlands and Sweden underline their shared views and values in the discussion on the architecture of the EMU', 5 March 2018, available at http://www.government.se/statements/2018/03/finance-ministers-from-denmark-estonia-finland-ireland-latvia-lithuania-the-netherlands-and-sweden/ (accessed 7 March 2018).

Oliver, T. (2016) 'European and international views on Brexit', *Journal of European Public Policy* 23(9): 1321–28.

Paterson, W.E. (2011) 'The reluctant hegemon: Germany moves center-stage in the European Union', *JCMS: Journal of Common Market Studies* 49(Annual Review): 57–75.

Quaglia, L. (2010) 'Completing the single market in financial services: the politics of competing advocacy coalitions', *Journal of European Public Policy* 17(7): 1007–23.

Quaglia, L., Howarth, D. and Liebe, M. (2016) 'The political economy of European capital markets union', *JCMS: Journal of Common Market Studies* 54(Annual Review): 185–203.

Schild, J. (2017) 'Französische Europapolitik unter Emmanuel Macron. Ambitionen, Strategien, Erfolgsbedingungen', *Integration* 40(3): 177–92.

Schild, J. (2018) 'Germany and France at cross purposes: the case of banking union', *Journal of Economic Policy Reform* 21(2): 102–17.

Schimmelfennig, F. (2018) 'Brexit: differentiated disintegration in the European Union', *Journal of European Public Policy* 25(8): 1154–73.

Schönberger, C. (2012) 'Hegemonie wider Willen: Zur Stellung Deutschlands in der Europäischen Union', *Merkur: Deutsche Zeitschrift für Europäisches Denken* 66(1): 1–8.

Sinn, H.-W. (2017) 'Die Bedeutung des Brexit für Deutschland und Europa', *Frankfurter Allgemeine Zeitung*, 16 March.

Spiegel online (2017) 'A trans-Atlantic turning point', 29 May 2017, available at http://www.spiegel.de/international/germany/merkel-and-trump-a-trans-atlantic-turning-point-a-1149757.html (accessed 30 October 2017).

The Guardian (2008) 'UK blocking European Congo force', 11 December, available at https://www.theguardian.com/world/2008/dec/12/congo-european-union-foreign-policy (accessed March 2017).

The Guardian (2017) 'Exclusive: macron pledges pragmatism and cooperation with post-Brexit Britain', 22 June 2017, available at https://www.theguardian.com/world/2017/jun/21/exclusive-macron-pledges-pragmatism-and-cooperation-with-post-brexit-britain (accessed 23 July 2017).

The Telegraph (2011) 'Britain blocks EU plans for "operational military headquarters"', 18 July, available at http://www.telegraph.co.uk/news/worldnews/europe/eu/8645749/Britain-blocks-EU-plans-for-operational-military-headquarters.html (accessed 26 July 2017).

Vollaard, H. (2014) 'Explaining European disintegration', *JCMS: Journal of Common Market Studies* 52(5): 1142–59.

Webber, D. (2014) 'How likely is it that the European Union will *Dis*integrate? A critical analysis of competing theoretical perspectives', *European Journal of International Relations* 20(2): 341–65.

Weber, S. (1996) 'Counterfactuals, past and future', in A. Belkin and P. Tetlock (eds.), *Counterfactual Thought Experiments in World Politics*, Princeton: Princeton University Press, pp. 268–88.

Zunneberg, C. (2017) 'What are the dynamics between EU heavyweights in the face of Brexit?' European Council on Foreign Relations, Commentary, 16 August.

Putting Brexit into perspective: the effect of the Eurozone and migration crises and Brexit on Euroscepticism in European states

Paul Taggart ⓘ and Aleks Szczerbiak ⓘ

ABSTRACT

This paper examines the link between recent EU crises and the development of party-based Euroscepticism across Europe. It draws on data from expert surveys with qualitative data to outline the way in which we can empirically see the link between the impacts of the crises in European states, and how far, and in what ways, Euroscepticism has been mobilized by political parties in those states. It identifies four main frames through which the EU is contested in European states which focus on: economic factors, immigration, democracy/sovereignty and national factors. It also shows that there has been a clear difference between the impacts of the different crises. While the Eurozone crisis had a particularly powerful effect in the party systems of those countries most affected by the bailout packages and the migration crisis had a particularly strong effect on party politics in the post-communist states of central Europe, Brexit has had a very limited impact on national party politics, although this may change in the longer-term.

1. Introduction

The EU is often portrayed as being in crisis (Habermas 2012; Ross 2011). Recent years have seen a veritable explosion in commentaries on the EU that have exemplified this narrative. For a political project, it is remarkable how often its very core has been apparently under challenge. One of the ways that challenges to the European project have been manifested has been in the rise of Euroscepticism. And just as there has been an explosion in the crisis narrative about the EU, so there has been a similar dramatic expansion in studies focused on Euroscepticism since the first was published in 1998 (Leconte 2010; Leruth *et al.* 2017; Szczerbiak and Taggart 2008a; Taggart 1998).

In addition to the rise of Euroscepticism, the EU has faced a number of severe challenges in the past decade. The economic crisis engendered by collapse in the US housing market in 2008 and resulting in the Eurozone crisis from 2010 onwards has had major impacts on many states (Schimmelfennig 2015). In 2015, Southern European states experienced a huge upsurge in asylum seekers many from Syria and economic migrants which resulted in the collapse of some key aspects of EU migration policy with a response in autumn 2015, when the European Council met in an emergency session and issued a migrant relocation plan. Then, in June 2016 the UK voted in a referendum to leave the EU which provided a challenge for the UK in terms of negotiating the terms of 'Brexit' and a potential challenge for the EU itself as one of its major members opted to leave (Bulmer and Quaglia, 2018).

This paper is an attempt to trace the link between recent crises and the development of Euroscepticism, particularly in the realm of party politics. The paper draws on data from expert surveys to outline the way in which we can empirically see the link between the impacts of the crises in European states, and how far, and in what ways, Euroscepticism has been mobilized by political parties in those states. The data for the paper is drawn from two expert surveys that were conducted in 2015 and in 2017 that examined the impact of the Eurozone crisis, the migration crisis and Brexit on Euroscepticism on party politics across Europe. We do, of course, acknowledge that Brexit differs from the other two crises examined in this paper in that it is very much ongoing and one that, at the time of writing is still to fully play out. However, that is also true, to some extent of the other two crises and we still think that it is valuable to address all three at this stage.

After briefly reviewing the 'state of play' as far as (party) Euroscepticism studies is concerned and setting out the methodology employed, the rest of the paper is divided into two main parts. The first addresses the findings of our first expert survey conducted in 2015 which focused on impact of the Eurozone crisis on party Euroscepticism and preceded both the migration and Brexit crises. As well as presenting an overview of which parties took Eurosceptic positions we have also tried to capture a portrait of how the 'European issue' was framed in different states. These results serve a snapshot of 2015 and as a benchmark for us to start to assess how far the migration crisis and Brexit had an impact of the expression of Euroscepticism. The second part of the paper relates to qualitative judgements from our experts concerning the impact of the three crises on party Euroscepticism. It discusses the second set of data from our 2017 experts survey which revisits the question of the Eurozone crises to see what has changed in the subsequent two years, and also looks at the migration and Brexit crises. As well as setting out an overall framework of findings, the paper identifies four clusters of countries' party systems were there were particularly interesting responses to the Brexit crisis, particularly when the impact of this was re-inforced by or linked to the two earlier ones.

2. Euroscepticism, crises and political parties

There has been a veritable explosion of interest in Euroscepticism studies in recent years (Szczerbiak and Taggart 2017). That work has mainly focused on either Euroscepticism as expressed by political parties or Euroscepticism within public opinion. And we can consider the key findings in terms of those effects before the crises and those that specifically focus on crises effects in these two areas.

The work on public opinion has a long lineage and has very often focused on the link between support for/opposition to European integration and economic factors. The work of Eichenberg and Dalton (2007), Gabel and Whitten (1997), Christin (2005) and Mau (2005) shows that an individual's economic position can have an impact on their attitudes towards the EU. Recent work by Lubbers and Scheepers (2010) shows that there are important national differences in the structuring of Euroscepticism.

A number of studies have addressed the particular effects of global economic and the Eurozone crises. Serricchio *et al.* (2012: 61) examine the link between the global economic crisis and support for Euroscepticism and find that 'national identity and political institutions play an increasingly important role in explaining public Euroscepticism'. Gomez (2015) shows that during the crisis citizens at least partially blamed the EU for their economic conditions. There is, naturally enough, less work on Brexit effects. However, in a recent article investigating the link between Brexit and Euroscepticism De Vries (2017) shows that there is evidence that uncertainty caused by Brexit actually reinforced pro-EU attitudes. We can therefore draw from the literature on public opinion that Eurosceptic sentiment will vary between countries but that we can expect some changes in Euroscepticism in response to the crises.

For the literature that focuses on the party politics of Euroscepticism there has been considerable work on the positions of parties (Hooghe *et al.* 2002; Szczerbiak and Taggart 2008a; Taggart 1998). This has mainly focused on the way that parties expressing Euroscepticism map onto new, or across existing, cleavage patterns so amounting to heterogeneous cluster of parties. As parties expressing Euroscepticism have become more central to their party systems there has been a focus on the impacts of their Euroscepticism (Meijers 2017; Taggart and Szczerbiak 2013).

For the literature on parties there has been less explicit work on the impact of crises on their positions. The 2014 European Parliament (EP) elections saw increasing support for parties expressing Euroscepticism and the elections have become a focus for those looking at party positions on Europe (Hobolt and De Vries, 2016; Nicoli 2017; Treib 2014; Wilde *et al.* 2014). Hobolt and De Vries (2016) show that the economic crisis had a significant impact on the support for parties expressing Euroscepticism. De Vries (2017) has also done considerable work on this topic showing the relationship in the other direction in which she argues that parties play a significant role in cueing mass attitudes on Euroscepticism. And Rohrschneider and Whitefield (2016) have used a quantitative expert survey to compare Euroscepticism in Western and Eastern Europe as a result of the financial crisis and find that mainstream parties did not substantially change their positions on the EU opening up space for new Eurosceptic parties. This work shows that we can expect some sort of effect of crises but that there will be national variations.

The research that we are presenting here is deliberately designed to complement this existing literature. The existing research emphasizes that national variations will shape the sorts of responses to crises. What our study adds to this is to try to map the nature of that variation. The focus on political parties rather than public opinion stems from the fact that we view parties as partially both cause and effect of public Euroscepticism. The focus on national politics, rather than looking at the EP, is justified because, while the latter provide a useful comparative arena for researchers, we contend that the role of parties at the national level has a far greater impact on the politics of European integration at all levels. The use of qualitative data in this analysis is meant to complement the existing work using quantitative data and allows us to drill down into national contexts in a different manner.

3. Methods

The data for this paper is based on a qualitative analysis of two experts surveys conducted by the authors: in 2015 when we examined the impact of the Eurozone crisis on Euroscepticism on party politics across Europe; then again at the beginning of 2017 when we asked our experts to update this and add data on the impact of the migration crisis and Brexit (defined as the UK's June 2016 referendum vote to leave the EU). For this survey, we drew on the expertise of the 150-strong European Parties Elections and Referendums Network (EPERN).[1]

The two surveys were sent to at least one leading specialist on party Euroscepticism in every EU member state (in some cases two or three were consulted) together with Norway, Serbia and Switzerland with survey results analyzed and tabulated by the authors. Respondents were then asked to confirm and comment upon these findings. We are extremely grateful to all of our respondents, although, while we are deferring to them in terms of country-level data, analysis and interpretation of the comparative findings are our own.

This method of conducting expert surveys is associated with what Cas Mudde (2012) has termed the 'Sussex school' of (party) Euroscepticism studies which has provided the data for a vast amount of high quality, internationally recognized published scholarship on the topic, notably a comprehensive seminal two volume collection of case studies and comparative/theoretical papers published in 2008 (Szczerbiak and Taggart 2008a). In reviewing the strengths and weakness of the EPERN database and 'Sussex school' methodology, Mudde (2012: 202) noted: 'The main strength of the Sussex School is validity, i.e., depth, detail, and expertise. EPERN is made up of scholars who specialize in Euroscepticism in a specific country, which they know through and through.' There are problems with, and limitations to, using expert surveys as a method of deriving party positions on issues such as European integration (Budge 2000). Researchers have developed strategies to get around this by: using precise descriptive terms, consulting a range of experts, and measuring both variance of findings among them and from alternative measures (Steenbergen and Marks 2007). Our approach in this paper has been to focus on the quality, rather than number, of the expert(s) consulted, on recognized specialists who have been surveyed previously on Eurosceptic party positions and, therefore, have a clear understanding of what is expected when categorizing a party in this way. We clearly circumscribed: (i) the time period that we were asking them to comment upon and (ii) the crises that we were asking them to consider responses to; while trusting their expert judgements in, and asking open-ended questions about, the terms of outlining the ways in which party Euroscepticism was articulated.

4. Euroscepticism in contemporary Europe

In earlier work we have mapped the presence of Euroscepticism in European party systems which provided us with a benchmark of the shape of party Euroscepticism at the beginning of the 2000s (Szczerbiak and Taggart 2008a; Taggart and Szczerbiak 2004). The research here allowed us to present an update of this to offer a picture of party Euroscepticism in 2015–2017. This covers both 'Hard' and 'Soft' Euroscepticism but we did not in our suervey questions differentiate between these forms (Szczerbiak and Taggart 2008b).

In addition to the mapping of party-based Euroscepticism we asked our respondents to describe the terms in which Euroscepticism was expressed in each country. This provided an array of issues and topics and the main themes are summarized, along with an overview of which parties took Eurosceptic positions, in Table 1 below. This includes many parties that are very minor parties and others which command more support. We have also included (where possible) the level of support for each party in the most

Table 1. Party-based Euroscepticism and frames for 'Europe' in European states.

Country	Eurosceptic parties	% support in most recent national election[a]
Austria	1. Freedom Party of Austria	20.51
	2. Social Democratic Party of Austria	28.82
	3. Austrian People's Party	23.99
	4. Team Stronach	5.73
	5. Alliance for the Future of Austria	3.53
	Frames:	Immigration
		Economy
Belgium	1. Flemish Interest	3.67
	2. Workers' Party of Belgium	3.72
	3. New Flemish Alliance	20.26
	Frames:	Values
		Immigration
		Economy
Bulgaria	1. Attack	4.52
	2. National Front for the Salvation of Bulgaria	7.28[b]
	3. Bulgarian National Movement	–[c]
	4. Bulgarian Socialist Party	15.40
	5. Minor parties from 'new left'	–
	Frames:	Economy
Croatia	1. Human Shield	–[d]
	Frames:	Economy
		Democracy
		Turkey
		Environmental politics
Cyprus	1. Progressive Party of Working People (AKEL)	25.67
	2. Ecologist Movement	4.81
	Frames:	Economy
		Militarism & Neoliberalism
		Immigration
		Sovereignty
Czech Republic	1. Dawn of Direct Democracy	6.88
	2. Freedom and Direct Democracy	–[e]
	3. Party of Free Citizens	2.46
	4. Communist Party of Bohemia and Moravia	14.91
	5. Civic Democratic Party	7.72
	Frames:	Democracy
		Sovereignty
		Bureaucracy
		Economics
		Immigration
Denmark	1. Danish People's Party	21.1
	2. Liberal Alliance	7.5
	3. Red Green Alliance	7.8
	4. New Civic Party	–[f]
	Frames:	Economy
		Democracy
		Immigration
Estonia	1. Estonian Independence Party	0.2
	2. Conservative People's Party of Estonia	8.1
	Frames:	Immigration
		Democracy/Bureaucracy
Finland	1. Finns	17.65

(Continued)

Table 1. Continued.

Country	Eurosceptic parties	% support in most recent national election[a]
	Frames:	Immigration Economy Sovereignty
France	1. National Front	21.30
	2. French Communist Party	19.58
	3. Workers' Struggle	0.64
	4. Anti-capitalist Party	1.09
	Frames:	Militarism Economy Democratic deficit
Germany	1. Left Party	8.59
	2. Alternative for Germany	4.7
	3. New Democratic Party	1.5
	Frames:	Economy Democratic
Greece	1. Communist Party	5.55
	2. SYRIZA	35.46
	3. Independent Greeks	3.69
	4. Golden Dawn	6.99
	5. Greek Orthodox Rally	–[g]
	Frames:	Democracy Values Immigration
Hungary	1. Fidesz	44.87
	2. Jobbik	20.22
	Frames:	Economy Democracy
Ireland	1. Sinn Fein	13.8
	2. People Before Profit Alliance	3.9
	3. Socialist Party	–[h]
	4. Anti-Austerity Alliance (Socialist Workers' Party)	–[i]
	5. Renua Ireland	2.2
	6. Independents	–[j]
	Frames:	Economy Immigration
Italy	1. Five Star Movement	25.56
	2. Northern League	4.09
	3. Brothers of Italy	1.96
	Frames:	Values Immigration
Latvia	1. Green-Farmers Union	19.53
	2. National Alliance	16.61
	Frames:	Values
Lithuania	No clearly Eurosceptic parties	–
	Frames:	–
Luxembourg	1. Alternative Democracy Reform	6.64
	2. The Left	4.94
	3. Communist Party of Luxembourg	1.64

(Continued)

Table 1. Continued.

Country	Eurosceptic parties	% support in most recent national election[a]
Malta	*Frames:*	N/A
	No clearly Eurosceptic parties	–
Netherlands	*Frames:*	Economy
		Immigration
		Democracy/Sovereignty
		Environmentalism
	1. Freedom Party	13.1
	2. Socialist Party	9.1
	3. Party for the Animals	3.2
	4. Forum for Democracy	1.8
Norway	*Frames:*	Economy
		Sovereignty
		Democracy
	1. Centre Party	5.5
	2. Socialist Left Party	4.1
	3. Christian Democratic Party	5.6
	4. Liberal Party	5.2
	5. Progress Party	16.3
	6. Labour Party	30.8
Poland	*Frames:*	Economy
		National sovereignty
		Moral-cultural values
	1. Law and Justice	37.58
	2. KORWiN /Freedom party)	4.76
	3. Kukiz '15	8.81
Portugal	*Frames:*	Economy
		Democracy/European 'political class'
	1. Communist Party	8.25[k]
	2. Left Block	10.19
	3. FREE/Time to Move Forward	.73
	4. Democratic Republican Party	1.13
	5. Socialist Alternative Movement	–03[l]
	6. Portuguese Workers Communist Party	1.13
Romania	*Frames:*	Economic
		Democracy
		Values
		Immigration
	1. Greater Romania Party	1.18
	2. United Romania Party	2.95
Serbia	*Frames:*	National Issues (EU recognition of Kosovo, relations with Russia)
	1. Serbian Radical Party	8.10
	2. Democratic Party of Serbia	1.04
	3. Doors	2.28
Slovakia	*Frames:*	Economy
		Values
		Sovereignty
	1. Slovak National Party	8.64
	2. Freedom and Solidarity	12.10
	3. Christian Democratic Movement	4.94

(Continued)

Table 1. Continued.

Country	Eurosceptic parties	% support in most recent national election[a]
	4. Ordinary People	11.03
	5. Nova	_[m]
	6. People's Party	8.04
	7. We are the Family	6.63
	Frames:	Economy
Slovenia	1. United Left	5.97
	2. Solidarity	_[n]
	3. Slovenian National Party	2.2
	Frames:	Economy
Spain	1. United Left (IU)	_[o]
	2. Podemos	21.15
	Frames:	Democracy
		Migration
		Women's Issues
Sweden	1. Sweden Democrats	12.9
	2. Left Party	5.7
	3. Feminist Initiative (No longer ES)	3.1
	Frames:	Immigration and Asylum
		Economy
Switzerland	1. Swiss People's Party	29.4
	2. Ticino League	1.0
	3. Movement of Genevan Citizens	0.3
	4. Swiss Democrats	0.1
	5. Freedom Party of Switzerland/Autopartei	–
	Frames:	Sovereignty
		Immigration
United Kingdom	1. Conservative Party	
	2. UKIP	
	Frames:	Economy
		Immigration

[a]Elections: Austria 2013; Belgium 2014; Bulgaria 2014; Cyprus 2016; Czech Republic 2013; Denmark 2015; Estonia 2015; Finland 2015; France 2017 (first round presidential); Germany 2013; Greece (September) 2015; Hungary 2014; Ireland 2016; Italy 2013; Latvia 2014; Luxembourg 2013; Netherlands 2017; Norway 2013; Poland 2015; Portugal 2015; Romania 2016; Serbia 2016; Slovakia 2016; Slovenia 2014; Spain (Congress of Deputies – 2016); Sweden 2014; Switzerland (federal) 2015; United Kingdom 2017.
[b]Stood in 2014 elections in alliance with Bulgarian National Movement.
[c]See footnote above.
[d]Not yet contested national election.
[e]Not yet contested national election.
[f]Not yet contested national election.
[g]Did not contest election.
[h]Stood in 2014 elections in alliance as part of Anti-Austerity Alliance – People before Profit Alliance.
[i]Stood in 2014 elections in alliance as part of Anti-Austerity Alliance – People before Profit Alliance.
[j]Various.
[k]Contested 2015 election as part of Unitary Democratic Coalition with Ecology Party.
[l]Stood in 2015 election in alliance with the Labour Party.
[m]Stood in 2016 election in alliance with Ordinary People.
[n]Stood with Social Democrats but failed to have any candidates elected to Parliament.
[o]Stood in 2016 election in alliance with Podemos.
Source: Authors' analysis based on expert surveys.

recent national elections. This is to offer an indication of the importance of the parties but should not be cumultaed as an an aggregate vote share for Euroscepticism given the diversity of the agendas of these parties.

Looking comparatively across the range of data we can make three general observations. Firstly, with only two exceptions all the European states surveyed had Euroscepticism in their party systems. While it differed in strength and form, we can say that Euroscepticism was an almost universal feature of contemporary European party systems making it a near universal staple component of European politics. The two exceptions were Lithuania and Malta, and in the case of Malta, Euroscepticism has been present as a major component in the party system (the currently-governing Labour Party) in the past.

This ubiquity can be seen in two diametrically opposed ways. On the one hand, it can be seen as indicative of a 'problem' in the sense that the presence of Euroscepticism is a symptom of a developing malaise or an inherent existing unstable condition in European integration. An alternative view is that the development of opposition to European integration is indicative of the 'normalization' of the politics of European integration. In this view, the relative absence of opposition previously was more indicative of the permissive consensus and elite-driven nature of the process.

Secondly, Euroscepticism spans the ideological range (Hooghe *et al.* 2002; Taggart 1998), albeit in an uneven way. It exists in parties on the left and right and in established as well as by new political parties. What is perhaps more remarkable is the breadth of different party ideologies that can incorporate some form of Euroscepticism. There are, however, some political gaps in the representation of Euroscepticism and these come mainly on the centre-left and in the liberal party family. Our findings suggested that there did not appear to be any European parties in the social democratic or liberal traditions that expressed Euroscepticism.

Thirdly, Euroscepticism has come in from being an exclusively insurgent peripheral phenomenon to one that is expressed by parties of government and not only by smaller and non-governmental parties. While it has not always become a powerful force, across Europe Euroscepticism has shown that it has the capacity to enter the political mainstream and to become a position adopted by parties of government. Of course, in the most spectacular case the British Conservative Party represents a party of government that has a track record of sustained Euroscepticism but is the only major government party in the EU to have flirted with, and eventually embraced, Hard Euroscepticism as an important component of its ideology. What is notable is that none of these three observations is qualitatively different from what could be observed before these crises (Szczerbiak and Taggart 2008a).

5. 'Frames' of European integration

Using the results of our first expert survey conducted in 2015 we have tried to capture a portrait of how the 'European issue' is framed in different European states. The context of this survey was the fall-out from the Eurozone crisis and the focus was to establish whether and how party Euroscepticism had developed in light of its negative effects. These results serve as a snapshot of 2015 and benchmark for us to start to assess how far Brexit has had an impact on the expression of Euroscepticism. The timing of the survey, which extended into the autumn of 2015, meant that, although our focus was on economic factors, the migration crisis came through in some of the findings.

The observations that we can make based on the 2015 survey thus serve as an important precursor to the current state of party Euroscepticism. Euroscepticism is often portrayed as a monolithic phenomenon but there are ways in which this can be qualified. The key difference lay in the way in which the 'European' issue was framed in different states.

There has been work on the different frames for the European issue but this focuses primarily on the sort of justifications used for the positions taken (Helbling *et al.* 2010). However, given that framing approaches are much more linked to elites or the media, we are using the term is a different sense. We were asking our respondents to assess the general context of the way in which the European issue was framed in a more widespread sense. In many ways our use of frames combines the 'issue-frames' that are used in the literature on US politics (Jacoby 2000) and 'diagnostic frames' that are used in social movement literature (Benford and Snow 2000) to identify the source of injustice to effect mobilization. The malleability of the European issue allows it to be attached to an unusually wide range of policy and political issues that can be used in this way. As a consequence, we could identify what were four different 'frames' that seemed to shape the way in which Euroscepticism was expressed. These frames were not mutually exclusive. We asked whether respondents could identify which issues were most significant or salient in their cases. This was in line with the approach taken by Hobolt and De Vries (2016) identifying different 'bases' of Euroscepticism.

The first frame was economic factors. Unsurprisingly, the framing of Euroscepticism as a critique of the economic failings of European integration was extremely common in the 2015 survey. However, what is also notable is that this economic framing took very different forms. There were many Eurosceptic parties that focused on the EU's 'austerity' agenda. Parties like SYRIZA in Greece had a resonant critique of the EU for implementing what was felt to be a damaging policy of economic 'austerity' in these countries. In contrast parties like 'The Finns' in Finland opposed the EU for its bailout of countries like Greece. These were clearly contingent positions taken in response to the particularities of the Eurozone crises and the subsequent policies of the EU and the Eurozone countries in response to that crisis. There were also parties that were explicitly against the Euro, such as the radical right 'Alternative for Germany' and communist AKEL in Cyprus. For those expressing a wider economic critique of the EU, there was again something of a set of polar opposites. There were parties like the 'Left' Party in Germany and Fidesz in Hungary who criticized the EU for being too liberal and the French National Front which saw the Union as insufficiently protectionist while other parties like UKIP saw it as too protectionist.

The second frame was issue of immigration. As noted above, this frame had a particular resonance as the migration crisis grew in 2015. However, the importance of the migration issue for radical right parties preceded this in Western Europe. Immigration was of importance primarily for parties in Western Europe historically but there were cases in central and Eastern Europe, such as Hungary and the Czech Republic, where Euroscepticism was mobilized around immigration issues due to the migration crisis and the sudden salience of refugees and the politicization of this policy area.

The third frame was that of concerns about democracy and sovereignty. There was convergence around this as a frame in a number of cases. In practice, there were, of course, differences about whether democracy or sovereignty was the primary focus. A 'pure' democracy critique focused around the democratic deficit of the EU. A sovereignty critique focused on a loss of national sovereignty through EU membership. The two are not necessarily fused as there can be concerns about a loss of sovereignty whether or not the international organization in question is felt to be sufficiently or insufficiently democratic. However, in practice these concerns tended to overlap and reinforce each other with concerns about a loss of national sovereignty being heightened by concerns about the EU's democratic deficit.

The fourth frame captures those cases where there were nationally specific concerns around particular issues that fundamentally shaped the way that the EU was viewed. The two cases that exemplify this are the concerns in Cyprus about Turkey and the concerns in Serbia about the status of Kosovo. This illustrates that, in certain cases, there are conditions that are sui generis and cannot be fully captured in looking only for European-wide trends.

Taken as a whole, what the 2015 survey results showed us was that the Eurozone crisis had had an impact on party Euroscepticism, but that this impact was by no means monolithic. It was clear that some very different frames were being deployed in the service of Euroscepticism and that it was important to pay attention to the importance of different national contexts in shaping which frames were salient to Euroscepticism and playing a key role in determining the extent of Euroscepticism.

6. The impact of Brexit (and other crises) on Euroscepticism

The second part of our data relates to qualitative judgements from our experts concerning the impact of the three crises on Euroscepticism in the countries and this section discusses the results of the second expert survey conducted in 2017. The survey returned to the data generated in 2015 and, in most cases, we asked the experts if the situation had changed since 2015 and to comment on whether the migration crisis and the Brexit crisis had had any impact on the articulation of Euroscepticism within their national party systems. Table 2 below provides a summary where we have attempted to collate and put those comments in a comparative frame. The differentiation of low, medium and high impacts of crises on Euroscepticism is derived from the authors' judgement based on the responses from country experts to open-ended questions which were then validated by the experts themselves. The

Table 2. The impact of Eurozone crisis, migration crisis and Brexit on party-based Euroscepticism in European states.

	EZ Crisis Impact	Migration Crisis Impact	Brexit Impact
Belgium	Low	Low	Low
Bulgaria	Low	High	Low/Medium
Croatia	Low	Low	Low
Cyprus	Medium	Medium	Low/Medium
Czech Republic	Medium	Medium	Low
Denmark	Low/ Medium	Low	Medium
Estonia	Low	Low/Medium	Low
Finland	Medium	Low	Low
France	Medium	Medium	Medium
Germany	Medium	Low	Low
Greece	High	High	Medium
Hungary	Low	High	Low
Ireland	High	Low	High
Italy	Medium	Medium	Low
Latvia	Low	Low	Low
Lithuania	Low	–	–
Luxembourg	Low	–	–
Malta	Low	Low	Low
Netherlands	Medium	Medium	Low
Norway	Medium	Low	Low/ Medium
Poland	Medium	Medium/High	Low/Medium
Portugal	Medium/High	Low	Low
Romania	Low	Low	Low
Serbia	Low	Low	Low
Slovakia	Low	Meidum	Low
Slovenia	Medium	Low	Low
Spain	High	Low	Low
Sweden	Low	Low	Low
Switzerland	Low	Low	Low

Source: Authors' analysis based on expert surveys.

points of comparison are with other countries rather than against an objective set of benchmarks.

Our expectation is that the three crises would play out somewhat differently in terms of domestic party politics. We would have expected the Eurozone crisis to have the greatest salience in the countries that were either on the receiving end of bailout conditionality or which were the most significant funders of the bailout packages. We would have expected the migration crisis to have the greatest salience in countries that were 'front-line states' in terms of migrant destinations, or where the prospect of (further) influxes of EU-mandated Muslim migrants either reinforced what was already a salient domestic issue or where Muslim migration raised concerns about EU-enforced multiculturalism. Our expectation of the impact of Brexit would be much more diffuse and low-key in the short-term at least given the lack of obvious 'winners' and 'losers' and elite-level nature of the Article 50 negotiations; rather we would expect it to be assimilated into existing Eurosceptic narratives. The longer-term effects would depend on whether Brexit was perceived to be a 'success' and how transferable the British experience was felt to be to other cases.

Our main finding is that there has been a clear difference between the impacts of the different crises. The Eurozone crisis had a particularly powerful effect, perhaps unsurprisingly, in the party systems of those countries most affected by the bailout packages: Germany, Greece and Ireland (to a lesser extent, Slovakia, Finland, Spain, Portugal). The migration crisis had a particularly strong effect on party politics in the post-communist states of central Europe (Poland, Hungary, Slovakia, Czech Republic), and also Bulgaria – but, interestingly, not most of the post-communist Balkan EU members (Croatia, Romania, Slovenia) and candidates (Serbia), nor the post-Soviet Baltic states.

The UK's June 2016 referendum vote to leave the EU, on the other hand, had a very limited impact on national party politics, particularly when compared with these two earlier EU crises. Its main effect was to re-inforce and legitimize existing 'Eurosceptic narratives, rather than lead to an increase in Eurosceptic party politics overall. This was not surprising. Beyond the immediate news impact of the actual referendum vote, Brexit was a rather distant and abstract process, with little apparent popular resonance – certainly compared with the two earlier crises which, in some countries at least, appeared to have a powerful public salience and perceived impact upon many people's day-to-lives. The survey was conducted before Article 50 was invoked and this meant that EU states had not formally reacted to Brexit. However, the initial nature of the process appeared to suggest that it would be complicated, elite-driven and multi-institutional, and therefore have low public resonance throughout the Brexit negotiations; except in Britain, of course, where it has dominated and over-shadowed other political issues.

Within this overall framework it is possible to identify four clusters of countries' party systems were there were particularly interesting responses to the Brexit crisis, particularly when the impact of this was reinforced by or linked to the two earlier crises. Firstly, the 'Visegrad Four' post-communist Central European states – the Czech Republic, Hungary, Poland and Slovakia – formed a significant, distinctive bloc in terms of the major impact of the European migration crisis. Although the Eurozone crisis had little impact on party politics in these countries (notwithstanding helping to bring down a Slovak government in 2011) and the Brexit referendum simply re-affirmed existing Eurosceptic narratives, the migration crisis did lead to a significant re-framing of the way that the EU was debated in these states, leading to a sharpening of Euroscepticism among mainstream political actors.

The notion of EU accession representing a historical-civilizational choice was a key factor in explaining why these countries voted overwhelmingly in 2003 accession referendums to join the EU and why it was very difficult for Eurosceptics to develop convincing narratives that appeared to go against the logic of the post-communist transformation process. However, in the view of its critics, by forcing these countries to adopt multi-culturalism, the EU's migrant relocation scheme raised significant doubts about whether the elites and publics in these countries were still making the same civilizational choices as their West European counterparts. This brought (Soft) Euroscepticism into the core of the party system involving not just right-wing conservative parties such as Law and Justice in Poland and Fidesz in Hungary, but centre-left governing parties such as the Czech Social Democrats and the social democratic Smer (Direction) party in Slovakia. On the other hand, in the Baltic republics security continued to trump all other considerations while in the Western Balkan 'front line' states the greater concern was that the EU managed the flows and shared the burden of migration rather than opposing compulsory migrant relocation in principle.

Secondly, there were a number of West European states were the three crises appeared to have had a significant and ongoing impact on the development of support for Eurosceptic parties. In Austria, Norbert Hofer, the presidential candidate of the Eurosceptic Freedom Party performed very well in the 2016 election, only defeated in a re-run second round run-off, and the party won more than one-fifth of the vote in the country's 2017 parliamentary election. The Eurozone crisis and the migration crisis both had the effect of crystallizing the Freedom Party's Euroscepticism but also, because of the direct impacts of both crises on Austria with a relatively large intake of migrants, also appeared to move the centrist Social Democrats and Christian Democrats to adopt a more critical tone towards the EU. The Brexit crisis also had an initial effect of bringing 'Oxit' into the political lexicon although subsequently all Austrian parties, even the Soft Eurosceptic ones, moved to a position of clarifying their support for EU membership in principle.

Denmark had a strong tradition of Eurosceptic public opinion and single issue parties and movements, and a propensity for EU referendums. Consequently, although Brexit and the two other crises only appeared to have a moderate impact on party Euroscepticism, the country had a strong Eurosceptic party on the radical right, the Danish People's Party, which was pushing for a 'British solution' and wanted a referendum to leave the EU. A new and reasonably well-supported right-wing Eurosceptic grouping, the New Civic Party, also emerged in 2016 and called for an EU membership referendum and for the Union to be re-focused solely on to free trade.

Italy had a large, radical anti-establishment Eurosceptic party in the Five Star Movement (Conti and Memoli 2015), which performed strongly in elections, and another medium-sized radical right Eurosceptic grouping, the Northern League. Party Euroscepticism in Italy was given much greater salience and opportunity by the Eurozone crisis, and sustained by the migration crisis, where the EU was accused even by mainstream parties of abandoning Italy. However, the main impact of the Brexit crisis appeared to be introducing the new word 'Italexit' into the political lexicon, although when they discussed this concept Eurosceptic parties in Italy referred mainly to leaving the Eurozone rather than the EU itself.

Thirdly, in some states where the two earlier crises boosted party Euroscepticism, the impact of the Brexit was not, or did not appear to be, as significant as some commentators expected. The Eurosceptic parties in question actually appeared to lose ground electorally – or, at least, did not match earlier expectations – and subsequently downplayed their opposition to European integration. France, for example, had a strong Eurosceptic party on the radical right, the National Front, and some smaller Soft Eurosceptic ones on the radical left. All three crises provided an impetus for the National Front: the Eurozone crisis created space for their Euroscepticism to flourish; the migration crisis allowed the increased focus on security to mesh with the party's policy on border control; and the Brexit crisis allowed it argue that 'Frexit' was clearly possible and galvanized the issue of a referendum on EU membership for the party. Eurosceptic candidates of left and right won a sizeable share in the first round of the April/May 2017 French presidential election. However, although National Front leader Marine Le Pen secured over one-third of the votes in the second round run-off, this was below expectations and actually rowed back from emphasizing Euroscepticism as the campaign progressed.

The Eurozone crisis was essential for the emergence and initial electoral success of the radical right Eurosceptic 'Alternative for Germany' party (Arzheimer 2015; Decker 2016), and also reinforced the Euroscepticism of the radical 'Left' party. However, while the migration crisis shifted the Alternative for Germany's policy focus, this came out more as anti-immigration than Eurosceptic and the party did little to tie these two issues together. Moreover, although both the 'Alternative for Germany' and 'Left' used the Brexit vote to legitimize their existing opposition to EU integration and, although the former emerged unexpectedly as the third largest party, it actually had little salience in the September 2017 federal election.

In Greece, Eurosceptic parties could be found on both the radical left – SYRIZA and the Communist Party – and right: the Independent Greeks, the neo-fascist Golden Dawn and (before it started to wane) the radical right Greek Orthodox Rally. Not surprisingly, the Eurozone crisis had a substantial impact on the Greek party system and led to major debates about, and criticisms of, the process that led to the country's economic settlement with the EU. Similarly, the migration issue led to a particularly intense debate around accusations that the EU was not doing enough to help Greece and was proving incapable of handling another crisis. However, although Brexit contributed to the general sense of uncertainty about the future of the EU it did not have the same impact as the two earlier crises. Indeed, over time SYRIZA also became somewhat less Eurosceptic; although, given that it was the main governing party after 2015, this could have been part of what Sitter (2001) (writing about the Scandinavian countries) termed the 'government-opposition' dynamic, whereby previously Eurosceptic opposition parties often became more pro-EU when they entered office and vice versa (Taggart and Szczerbiak 2013).

Given the previous electoral successes of the radical right Eurosceptic Freedom Party of Geert Wilders, there was also considerable interest in how the Brexit crisis would play out in the Netherlands. Earlier, the Eurozone crisis had some impact when the Freedom Party attempted to use it to bolster its arguments about sovereignty, while the radical left (Soft Eurosceptic) Socialist Party also objected to the costs of the bailout packages. The Freedom Party also used the migration crisis to call for the closing of the Dutch borders. However, although the party originally lauded the UK's 'independence day', Brexit barely featured as one of the themes in the Freedom Party's March 2017 parliamentary election campaign when, although it slightly increased its share of the vote and remained the main opposition grouping, the party performed below expectations.

Fourthly, there was at least one interesting case where earlier crises had boosted party Euroscepticism but this actually appeared to go into reverse as a result of the Brexit crises, namely: Ireland. The Eurozone crisis pushed Euroscepticism to the fore of the Irish party system and transformed the salience of these issues in the country's political debate. However, Brexit appeared to dramatically reduce party-based Euroscepticism in Ireland due to: the economic uncertainty that it was felt to generate; the new opportunities it presented for Irish 'reunification' and for Ireland to act as a bridge between the UK and EU; and the fact that British Hard Euroscepticism came to be associated closely with English nationalism. Interestingly, there was also some evidence that similar dynamics appeared to be at work in terms of public opinion across the whole of the EU (De Vries 2017).

Taken together, of all the three crises, it is clear that Brexit had the least impact, although we can also see that there were very different patterns of impact. This reflected the variations of national contexts and party systems shaping the way in which European integration was contested as a political issue. It means that we need to be cautious about over-generalizing about trends and more assiduous in taking full account of national contexts in tracing reactions to European phenomena.

7. Conclusions: competing narratives and British exceptionalism?

This paper has examined the link between recent EU crises and party-based Euroscepticism across Europe. We have used expert surveys with qualitative data to outline the contemporary state of party-based Euroscepticism. It has shown the widespread but uneven nature of party-based Euroscepticism. Through doing this we have identified four main frames through which the EU is contested in European states which focus on: economic factors, immigration, democracy/sovereignty and national factors. We then examined the impact of the three crises on European states which have, again, demonstrated significant variation but overall a relative lack of impact of Brexit on Euroscepticism.

When considering the impact of Brexit it is also important to distinguish the short-term and long-term – and the dynamic effects of one of the largest member states leaving the EU on the organization, both in terms of perceptions and the reality of how it operates (or even survives) in the future. On the one hand, if the Brexit process is a relatively smooth one and Britain is, or appears to be, successful outside the EU bloc there is a possibility that it could be used as a model for other Eurosceptic parties who could then shift to adopting a (Hard) Eurosceptic stance. One the other hand, if it is not a success, or not perceived to be one, this could discourage Soft Eurosceptic parties from adopting a Hard Eurosceptic stance, and all kinds of Eurosceptics (especially Hard ones) from articulating their position (as appeared to be happening in Ireland).

However, there are two reasons why even then the perceived 'success' or 'failure' of Brexit may not lead to long-term changes in the levels, nature and salience party Euroscepticism. Firstly, unless developments are completely unambiguous the question of whether or not Brexit is a 'success' or 'failure' is likely to be highly contested, with any subsequent developments filtered and interpreted through the different narratives of Euroenthusiasts and Eurosceptics respectively. Secondly, even if the outcome is seen as more clear-cut, questions will still be raised about British exceptionalism and whether broader lessons can really be drawn; this is particularly likely to be the case if Brexit is a 'success'.

Note

1. EPERN was established in 2000 originally as the 'Opposing Europe Research Network', a network of scholars researching the comparative party politics of Euroscepticism. It then broadened its intellectual focus out to encompass the domestic politics of European integration and its impact on parties, elections and referendums more generally, with the study of Euroscepticism one (albeit important) strand within that; although in recent years, EPERN's main research focus has returned once again to party Euroscepticism. See: http://www.sussex.ac.uk/sei/research/europeanpartieselectionsreferendumsnetwork.

Disclosure statement

No potential conflict of interest was reported by the authors.

Funding

This work was supported by an Economic and Social Research Council (ESRC) 'UK in a Changing Europe' programme commissioning grant [PO 4030006666]. All the data produced is included in the published article.

ORCID

Paul Taggart ⓘ http://orcid.org/0000-0002-1535-3015
Aleks Szczerbiak ⓘ http://orcid.org/0000-0003-4389-9557

References

Arzheimer, K. (2015) 'The AFD: finally a successful right-wing populist Eurosceptic party for Germany?', *West European Politics* 38(3): 535–56.
Benford, R.D. and Snow, D.A. (2000) 'Framing processes and social movements: an overview and assessment', *Annual Review of Sociology* 26(1): 611–39.
Budge, I. (2000) 'Expert judgements of party policy positions: uses and limitations in political research', *European Journal of Political Research* 37: 103–13.
Bulmer, S. and Quaglia, L. 2018. 'The politics and economics of Brexit', *Journal of European Public Policy* 25(8), doi:10.1080/13501763.2018.1467957.
Christin, T. (2005) 'Economic and political basis of attitudes towards the EU in Central and East European Countries in the 1990s', *European Union Politics* 6(1): 29–57.
Conti, N. and Memoli, V. (2015) 'The emergence of a new party in the Italian party system: rise and fortunes of the Five Star movement', *West European Politics* 38(3): 516–34.
De Vries, C.E., (2017) 'Benchmarking Brexit: How the British decision to leave shapes EU public opinion', *JCMS: Journal of Common Market Studies* 55: 38–53.

Decker, F. (2016) 'The "alternative for Germany:" factors behind its emergence and profile of a new right-wing populist party', *German Politics and Society* 34(2): 1–16.

Eichenberg, R.C. and Dalton, R.J. (2007) 'Post-Maastricht blues: the transformation of citizen support for European integration, 1973–2004', *Acta Politica* 42(2-3): 128–52.

Gabel, M. and Whitten, G.D. (1997) 'Economic conditions, economic perceptions, and public support for European integration', *Political Behavior* 19(1): 81–96.

Gomez, R. (2015) 'The economy strikes back: support for the EU during the great recession', *JCMS: Journal of Common Market Studies* 53(3): 577–92.

Habermas, J. (2012) *The Crisis of the European Union: A Response*, Cambridge: Polity.

Helbling, M., Hoeglinger, D. and Wüest, B. (2010) 'How political parties frame European integration', *European Journal of Political Research* 49(4): 495–521.

Hobolt, S.B. and De Vries, C. (2016) 'Turning against the union? The impact of the crisis on the Eurosceptic vote in the 2014 European Parliament elections', *Electoral Studies* 44: 504–14.

Hooghe, L., Marks, G. and Wilson, C.J. (2002) 'Does left/right structure party positions on European integration?', *Comparative Political Studies* 35(8): 965–89.

Jacoby, W.G. (2000) 'Issue framing and public opinion on government spending', *American Journal of Political Science* 44: 750–67.

Leconte, C. (2010) *Understanding Euroscepticism*, Basingstoke: Palgrave Macmillan.

Leruth, B., Startin, N. and Usherwood, S. (eds) (2017) *The Routledge Handbook of Euroscepticism*, London: Routledge.

Lubbers, M. and Scheepers, P. (2010) 'Divergent trends of euroscepticism in countries and regions of the european Union', *European Journal of Political Research* 49(6): 787–817.

Mau, S. (2005) 'Europe from the bottom: assessing personal gains and losses and its effects on EU support', *Journal of Public Policy* 25(3): 289–311.

Meijers, M.J. (2017) 'Contagious Euroscepticism: The impact of Eurosceptic support on mainstream party positions on European integration', *Party Politics* 23(4): 413–423.

Mudde, C. (2012) 'The comparative study of party-based Euroscepticism: the Sussex versus the North Carolina School', *East European Politics* 28(2): 193–202.

Nicoli, F. (2017) 'Hard-line Euroscepticism and the Eurocrisis: evidence from a panel study of 108 elections across Europe', *JCMS: Journal of Common Market Studies* 55 (2): 312–31.

Rohrschneider, R. and Whitefield, S. (2016) 'Responding to growing European Union-skepticism? The stances of political parties toward European integration in Western and Eastern Europe following the financial crisis', *European Union Politics* 17(1): 138–61.

Ross, G. (2011) *The European Union and its Crises: Through the Eyes of the Brussels' Elite*, New York, NY: Palgrave Macmillan.

Schimmelfennig, F. (2015) 'Liberal intergovernmentalism and the euro area crisis', *Journal of European Public Policy* 22(2): 177–95.

Serricchio, F., Tsakatika, M. and Quaglia, L. (2012) 'Euroscepticism and the global financial crisis', *JCMS: Journal of Common Market Studies* 51(1): 51–64.

Sitter, N. (2001) 'The politics of opposition and European integration in Scandinavia: is Euro-scepticism a government-opposition dynamic?', *West European Politics* 24(4): 22–39.

Steenbergen, M.R. and Marks, G. (2007) 'Evaluating expert judgements', *European Journal of Political Research* 46: 347–66

Szczerbiak, A. and Taggart P. (2017) 'Research on Euroscepticism; the state of the art', in B. Leruth, N. Startin and S. Usherwood (eds.), *The Routledge Handbook of Euroscepticism*, London: Routledge, 11–21.

Szczerbiak, A. and Taggart, P. (eds) (2008a) *Opposing Europe? The Comparative Party Politics of Euroscepticism: 2 Vols*, Oxford: Oxford University Press.

Szczerbiak, A. and Taggart, P. (2008b) 'Theorizing party-based Euroscepticism: problems of definition, measurement and causality', in Aleks Szczerbiak and Paul Taggart (eds.), *Opposing Europe? The Comparative Party Politics of Euroscepticism: Volume 2: Comparative and Theoretical Perspectives*, Oxford: Oxford University Press, 238–262.

Taggart, P. (1998) 'A touchstone of dissent: Euroscepticism in contemporary Western European party systems', *European Journal of Political Research* 33(3): 363–88.

Taggart, P. and Szczerbiak, A. (2004) 'Contemporary euroscepticism in the party systems of the European Union candidate states of Central and Eastern Europe', *European Journal of Political Research* 43(1): 1–27.

Taggart, P. and Szczerbiak, A. (2013) 'Coming in from the cold? Euroscepticism, government participation and party positions on Europe', *JCMS: Journal of Common Market Studies* 51(1): 17–37.

Treib, O. (2014) 'The voter says no, but nobody listens: causes and consequences of the Eurosceptic vote in the 2014 European elections', *Journal of European Public Policy* 21 (10): 1541–54.

Wilde, P., Michailidou, A. and Trenz, H.J. (2014) 'Converging on Euroscepticism: online polity contestation during European Parliament elections', *European Journal of Political Research* 53(4): 766–783.

Taking back control: the political implications of Brexit

Andrew Gamble

ABSTRACT

The consequences of the BREXIT vote in June 2016 will take many years to be fully understood. The focus of the debate has shifted from whether there should be a BREXIT at all to what kind of BREXIT the UK should now seek to achieve. The result of the referendum and the Brexit election of 2017 has already had a profound effect on all the UK's main political parties, and has raised difficult questions about Britain's role in the world, its governance, its political economy, and the future of the United Kingdom. This article will assess the changes which have already taken place, and will ask whether BREXIT will have lasting consequences for British politics and British government. Will it come to be seen as a watershed in the political development of the UK, or only an episode in a continuous process of evolution?

Introduction

The vote to leave the European Union in the referendum held on 23 June 2016 initiated a process which may take many years to complete, and is unlikely ever to be completed in the way that many Leavers hope. The complexity of the task of disentangling the UK from the European Union after forty years of membership has become clear in the period since the referendum (see Bulmer and Quaglia 2018). Whether it will come to be viewed as a major watershed in modern British history or merely an episode in the process of the UK's evolving relationship with the rest of Europe is unclear. There is unlikely ever to be political agreement on the consequences of Brexit, or on whether in the long-run it was harmful or beneficial. The vote undermined one of the pillars of the elite consensus since the 1960s, namely that the UK's future lay in being a full member of the European Union. The referendum has unleashed a new dynamic in British politics.

Many Leavers have hailed Brexit as a new 1688, a second 'Glorious' Revolution restoring English liberties and national self-confidence (Patient 2017).

Other commentators see it as a new 1534, a second Act of Supremacy over-throwing foreign jurisdiction over England (Hattersley 2017). Despite the his-torical inaccuracy of these comparisons their purpose is to signal that Brexit is the moment when the United Kingdom, or rather England, regains its sover-eignty, making all things possible again. The people reclaim the right to deter-mine how the country should be governed, the character of its political arrangements, and its place in the world. This romantic notion of sovereignty is associated with Enoch Powell. What mattered most to him was the ability of a sovereign Parliament to determine the laws, not what the content of those laws might be. The people might vote misguidedly for socialism, but that was a secondary concern, provided they retained the power to elect representa-tives to a sovereign Parliament. It is a powerful vision, and was once shared by many on the Left. But its emphasis on agency and its neglect of structural constraints risks overrating the importance of Brexit and raises expectations too high about the opportunities in a post-Brexit future. 1534 and 1688 are key dates in the story of the expansion of England from small kingdom on the fringes of Europe to far flung colonial and commercial empire. No such expansion looks possible today. This Brexit vision also exaggerates the extent of the UK's integration into Europe. The UK was already semi-detached from the European Union long before 2016. The vote for Brexit makes that status explicit, ridding the EU of an increasingly troublesome and obstructive member. From the Maastricht Treaty onwards it was clear that Britain was never going to be a full member of any new project for European integration, so the vote for Brexit while costly in the short term to both sides and the cause of much uncertainty, may ultimately lead to the working out of a more durable associate status for the UK with the EU, which removes some of the frictions but also preserves some of the benefits of Britain's 43 year membership.

This article discusses the vote itself, the fears and hopes of Remainers and Leavers, and how Brexit altered policy choices and helped unleash a new populist dynamic into British politics, which influenced the June 2017 general election, the first to take place after Brexit. It then considers some of the possible longer-term impacts Brexit may have on institutions and pol-icies which have made the United Kingdom distinctive in the past, such as its multinational political union, its party system, uncodified constitution, centra-lised governance, its Anglo-liberal political economy, and its post-imperial international role. Will Brexit reverse forty years of Europeanisation and con-vergence towards European norms, making the UK much more distinctively British again? Or will the convergence continue even post-Brexit?

The impact of the referendum

The Referendum result was narrow, but also clear. It was also unexpected. There had only been two nation-wide referendums before the Brexit vote, the first Referendum on whether to confirm membership of the European Community in 1975 and the vote on whether to replace the first past the post voting system in 2011. Both were comfortable victories for the status quo, and the experience of referendums in other democracies was that this was the normal outcome (Qvortrup 2005). Fear of the unknown meant that the argument 'why risk it?' Generally prevailed. The Remain campaign had many faults and its leaders made many misjudgements, but it was still able to count on the support of the bulk of the political establishment, and business leaders, as well as a formidable array of national and international experts and authorities, from the Bank of England to the IMF.

The vote was a major blow to the authority of the political class and the governing institutions of the state. It created a serious gap between Parliament and people, since although the people voted for Leave, there was a substantial majority among MPs for Remain. The Referendum was only advisory but could Parliament disregard such a clear 'instruction' from the electorate, especially when the Prime Minister had undertaken to respect the result? Most MPs concluded that they could not, but then faced another problem. No-one could be sure how to interpret that instruction, since there had been no formal manifestos and voters had many different reasons for voting as they did. The will of the people as to what kind of Brexit they wanted had to be interpreted by the Government and Parliament. It could not simply be assumed.

In the immediate aftermath of Brexit both major political parties were plunged into turmoil. David Cameron resigned immediately as Leader of the Conservative Party, triggering a leadership election, while Jeremy Corbyn faced a leadership challenge, after the resignation of most of his front bench team partly because of his lukewarm support for the Remain campaign. Both parties were forced to conduct leadership elections at the same time, which had never happened before. Both parties were shown to be deeply divided by the referendum result but in different ways. 59 per cent of voters who had supported Cameron only a year before at the 2015 general election had rejected his advice and voted Leave in 2016. For Labour 63 per cent of Labour voters had voted Remain and only 37 per cent Leave, but 70 per cent of Labour constituencies voted Leave (Hanretty 2016).

The leadership election in the Conservative party was brutal but quick. When Andrea Leadsom withdrew, Theresa May was left standing as the only serious candidate, and she was duly elected Leader and appointed Prime Minister without the need for a vote of Conservative members. The Labour party staged a much lengthier leadership election, which ended with the same result as in 2015, Corbyn winning by a comfortable margin. The Conservatives elected a Leader who had backed Remain despite a majority of Conservative voters and members having voted Leave, while

Labour confirmed in office a Eurosceptic who had voted against every EU treaty since 1983 despite a majority of Labour voters and still more members (87 per cent) having voted Remain.

Both parties had then to grapple with what Brexit meant. In 2016 voters were asked to choose between leaving and remaining in the European Union, but these terms were extremely vague and the rival campaigns interpreted them in many different ways. The Leave campaign could not agree on a unified campaign, so its campaign was run by two rival organisations, Vote Leave and Leave EU (Shipman 2016). At the time this was considered a weakness but it may have helped them to maximise their vote by delivering different messages to different groups of votes. Voters could choose between global Britain, which would be committed to free trade, low taxes, and deregulation and Britain First, a country in which immigration would be reduced to very low levels, and government would intervene to bring back manufacturing jobs and the close-knit communities of the past.

The Leave and Remain campaigns were both largely negative, Remainers warning of the dire economic consequences of Brexit, while Leavers highlighted the flood of new immigrants which would overwhelm the UK from Eastern Europe and from Turkey if the UK voted to stay in. The Remain campaign made few attempts to make a positive case for the ideal of European integration and the pooling of sovereignty. This contrasted with the Leave campaign which employed the old radical slogan 'take back control'. It portrayed a vision of Britain as once again an independent country in full control of its laws, its borders, and its money. Voters were told that Brexit would not only be cost-free but would also bring tremendous benefits, such as £350 million extra a week for spending on the NHS once the UK had ceased paying into the EU budget. This programme proved very popular and swayed many votes, although none of the Leaders of the Leave campaign making these promises was in a position to deliver them. They were not running as an alternative government, accountable to the electorate. This left a vacuum after the result was announced, since the actual Government comprised mostly of Remainers now had the responsibility to interpret the result and deliver Brexit.

What kind of Brexit?

The vacuum was filled by Theresa May. The Government announced it would deliver Brexit and Theresa May appointed a cabinet to do just that, finding important ministerial roles for three leading Brexiters, Boris Johnson, David Davis and Liam Fox. She achieved this by dividing the Foreign Office into three and creating two new departments, the Department for Exiting the European Union, and the Department for International Trade. But it took a long time before the new Government was ready to trigger Article 50 and commence the formal negotiations on the terms of exit. The actual start of negotiations was then further delayed because the Government called a general election. The formal negotiations only began a year after the vote.

The debate on the nature of Brexit became simplified as a choice between hard and soft Brexit. Hard Brexit, or clean Brexit, as many Leavers preferred to call it, was a maximalist position, defined as taking back control of laws, borders and money, quickly and smoothly. The most optimistic maximalists such as the group *Economists for Brexit* argued that Britain did not need a trade deal with the EU or anyone else. Britain would be best served by declaring unilateral free trade. It did not matter what other countries did. Britain would impose no tariffs of any kind on goods entering the UK market. If Britain did not need a trade deal with the EU its bargaining hand in the negotiations over the terms of separation under Article 50 would be immensely strengthened. A slightly softer version of this stance, favoured by Nigel Lawson among others, was that Britain did not need to negotiate a separate trade deal with the EU because it could rely on WTO rules. For its proponents this outcome would give the UK the maximum freedom to strike its own trade deals and to determine its own regulatory regime. Sacrificing some access to the single market would be a price worth paying to secure that.

This maximalist position was closely allied to the promotion of 'global Britain'. Brexit was an opportunity to complete the domestic revolution in policy which Margaret Thatcher had started, and which had been halted and partially reversed under Major, Blair and Cameron. Globalists wanted a return to a policy regime which promoted low taxes, de-regulation, a minimal state, and flexible labour markets. Britain after Brexit was said to have an exceptional opportunity to recover the commercial agility and entrepreneurial drive which it had displayed in the nineteenth century. Against a background of a slowing growth in international trade and a large and growing UK trade deficit (more than 7 per cent of GDP), the urgency for Britain outside the EU to recover its commercial elan was pressing. Liam Fox claimed that British business had grown fat and lazy. Exporting should not be thought of as an opportunity but as a duty (Fox 2016), a familiar refrain of ministers in the 1960s, before entry to the Common Market.

The other maximalist position on the Leave side was the nationalist position associated with UKIP. For nationalists Brexit meant above all the opportunity to take back control by radically reducing immigration (Dennison and Geddes 2018). Many Leave voters wanted to see a big reduction in the number of immigrants already in the UK. UKIP Leaders acknowledged that some immigration would have to continue after Brexit, but they wanted it to return to the levels of the early 1990s, no more than 30,000 or 40,000 a year, instead of the 300,000 which had become common in the years before the referendum, particularly following the decision of the Labour Government not to impose restrictions on the free movement of citizens of new member states such as Romania and Bulgaria after 2004. Immigration was a source of tension with the globalists in the Leave campaign, who wanted to emphasise the wider advantages of taking back control rather than making immigration the priority. It simmered during the campaign and burst out after the vote was won. Many prominent figures in the Leave campaign were openly disparaging of the desire of the nationalists to achieve a drastic reduction in immigration numbers, because of the effects this would have on the UK economy, which for the past fifteen years had become very dependent on immigrant labour. Strict control of immigration would undermine the flexible labour market and be inconsistent with the low tax, low regulation regime which the globalists sought.

The Remainers, who formed a majority in May's Cabinet, as well as a majority amongst Conservative MPs, mostly accepted the Referendum result but advocated a minimalist position on Brexit. Staying in the single market and the customs union was a greater priority than ending free movement. Britain's trade interests were best served by negotiating some form of associate status with the EU post Brexit to ensure the least possible damage to British trade and jobs. This could be secured by joining the European Economic Area, and securing a similar status to Norway, Iceland and Lichtenstein. Minimalists fear the short-term dislocation in trade and the scale of economic adjustment that a harder form of Brexit implies, and the long-term damage to the Conservative reputation for economic competence if there was a market collapse and another steep fall in the pound as a result of hard Brexit. They argue that the British growth model developed over three decades depends in part on a very flexible labour market and expanding employment. It only works if there are high levels of immigration. Bringing immigration down below 100,000 per annum will be hard to do without destroying many key sectors of the British economy. But they are aware that if immigration is not reduced to much lower levels, Brexit will be denounced as a hoax by a new generation of populists.

Another serious misgiving of the minimalists about the impact of Brexit is that it exchanges a very strong and stable trading relationship with the EU for a set of trade deals with other countries which may well involve even more loss of sovereignty. A trade deal with India for example may require the UK to accept a much higher level of Indian immigration. A trade deal with the US may require reductions in environmental standards and protections, and the opening up of the British public sector including the NHS to US firms. Against this they cited the proven advantages of the single market in raising prosperity and productivity. Many of the minimalists accepted the political difficulties and dangers of reversing or ignoring the Brexit decision. But as the full implications of leaving the EU became apparent, they pressed the Government to secure status quo transitional arrangements after 2019, while a long-term trade deal was negotiated. Because minimalists were often at best lukewarm about Brexit, and downbeat about the opportunities it brought the British economy, many Leavers accused them of seeking to sabotage Brexit, making the transitional arrangements permanent, so that Britain never leaves.

Theresa's May position has at times appeared to be both maximalist and minimalist, globalist and nationalist. This has often been an advantage for her. When she ran for Leader many Leavers were suspicious of her and did not vote for her, arguing that to be credible the new Leader of the Conservatives had to be a Leaver. Yet despite this it was Leavers who in the early period of her government were happier with May as Prime Minister than Remainers. The balance of government policy was tilted firmly towards the demands of the Leave campaign and the concerns of the 52 rather than the 48 per cent. In a series of speeches, at the Conservative party Conference in October 2016, and then definitively in her speech at Lancaster House in January 2017, May made it clear that she now accepted the result of the Referendum. Brexit meant Brexit. The vote on June 32rd 2016 had been clear and decisive and that meant Britain was leaving the EU. The Referendum vote she declared gave the government a mandate to implement Brexit. It was quite clear what the people had voted for, namely that Britain should be a sovereign nation again with full control of its own borders and laws. Trade and investment were secondary issues to be determined once Britain was sovereign again. Existing trade links could not be allowed to stand in the way.

May had concluded that this was the only strategy which was politically realistic. Immigration was crucial. To honour the Referendum result she had to deliver immigration control in a way which would be understood in those constituencies, particularly in the North and East of England, which had voted Leave. Her inflexibility began to alarm many minimalists, because her stance appeared to pay no heed to the grave risks to the economy and to the Union of a hard Brexit. But May and her advisers were more concerned with the political risks the Government would face if she failed to satisfy her maximalist wing whose concerns were amplified by the Conservative newspapers.

In pursuit of her strategy May reduced contact with representatives of business and downplayed their concerns, while still maintaining that she wanted a 'deep and special' partnership with the EU after Brexit, including a free trade deal. Donald Tusk, the president of the European Council, repeatedly warned that the UK could not cherry pick and must choose between a hard Brexit or no Brexit (Tusk 2017). If Britain wished to leave the EU in order to regain full control over its borders it could not expect to retain the privileged trading status which the single market conferred on member states. Yet Theresa May and several of the Brexiters in her Cabinet continued to maintain that Britain could take back control of its borders and still expect full access to the single market. It could achieve a frictionless exit. But although May flirted from time to time with this have cake and eat it approach, her basic position remained clear. She declared repeatedly that no deal was preferable to a bad deal, which many took to be a bluff, but a bluff which she might be forced to go through with and see Britain crash out of the EU without a deal of any kind. This did not worry the unilateral free trade globalists, but it caused consternation and dismay throughout business and the civil service as well as a large part of the Cabinet and the Conservative party, aware of what this could mean for the economy and for social cohesion, and for the Conservatives' reputation for economic competence.

The 2017 general election

When Article 50 was finally triggered in March 2017, May was riding high. The Conservative party had united behind her. She had won support from the pro-Brexit media of a kind which no Conservative Leader had enjoyed since Margaret Thatcher. She enjoyed approval ratings of plus 10. Jeremy Corbyn by contrast had an approval rating of minus 40. The Conservatives had a poll lead over Labour of more than twenty points, and in March it captured the Copeland constituency from Labour in a by-election, the first time a governing party had won a byelection since 1982 and in a seat which Labour had held since 1935. Despite her earlier denials that there would be an early general election the opportunity to win a personal mandate, increase her freedom of manoeuvre and be guaranteed office for a full five years, stretching comfortably beyond the point at which Britain would leave the EU in 2019, was too great to resist. An election was called for June 8th.

The election became the Brexit election, in two senses. Its outcome was heavily shaped by how people had voted in the Referendum, and the result was, like the Referendum, unexpected. Instead of increasing their overall majority the Conservatives lost the one they had, despite increasing their share of the vote and their total number of votes. May's authority was temporarily shattered. Her plans for a far-reaching reshuffle, had to be abandoned, and she had to sacrifice her two closest aides, Nick Timothy and Fiona Hill. Not only had the Conservatives inexplicably taken a step backwards, but they had allowed Labour with a populist left programme to make a big step forward. Labour's successful campaign and manifesto transformed the standing of Jeremy Corbyn, the party increased its vote share by ten percentage points, and had a net gain of 30 seats. The Conservatives had targeted Labour northern seats which had voted Leave and had a significant UKIP vote in 2015. The UKIP vote collapsed, but the Conservatives only picked up five of their target seats. 18 per cent of the UKIP vote went back to Labour, which also polled strongly amongst the young, graduates, ethnic groups and in big cities, especially London. The surge of young voters and Remain voters for Labour saw the capture of traditional Conservative seats including Kensington and Canterbury.

The Conservatives still won sixty more seats than Labour, and they were able to stay in government by concluding a confidence and supply agreement with the pro-Brexit Democratic Unionists in Northern Ireland. But the election transformed the political situation, and made May's position highly precarious. The difficulty of carrying through a hard Brexit of the kind she had favoured before the election was made much more difficult. The hard Brexit wing of the Conservatives was already emboldened and ready to punish any backsliding. But now the anti-Brexit wing of the Conservatives was emboldened too. Both had enough votes to bring her Government down and so force concessions. Her negotiating hand in Brussels was substantially weakened, and it was questioned whether she could command a majority in Parliament to get through essential Brexit legislation.

The election showed the impact of Brexit. It confirmed a realignment of voters across traditional party lines, and confirmed that the Referendum had unleashed some new and destabilising forces in British politics. The victory of the Leave campaign which relied in part on populist appeals against the political class and established authority and expertise, created conditions in which other forms of populism could succeed. In 2017 the unexpected beneficiary of the new populist mood was Corbyn's Labour party. Corbyn's status as an outsider and his populist manifesto sparked a Labour surge. The irony of his success was that it owed much to Remain voters, yet the manifesto had been vague over what Labour's precise policy towards Brexit was. It managed to suggest that Labour would end free movement, but would also negotiate the fullest possible access to the single market and would grant EU citizens their full rights. But it soon became clear after the election that Jeremy Corbyn still believed that Britain should leave the EU and that part of leaving was leaving the single market and regaining control of immigration. His position was very close to that of the Government, and a long way from his enthusiastic young supporters who had turned out to vote Labour in record numbers. Under pressure from the party Labour's official position was later modified and Labour became committed to staying in the single market and customs union during the transition period, as well as arguing that no arbitrary time limit should be placed on how long that should be. In 2018 it became committed to staying in a customs union in perpetuity. But the commitment to respect the referendum result and leave the EU remained Labour's official position. The leadership opposed calls for a second referendum.

Negotiations with the EU began in earnest after the election. British ministers still hoped that the EU would agree to discuss the terms of the divorce settlement alongside a future trade deal, and that this could all be agreed quickly. The EU however insisted that any discussion of a trade deal could only begin once the 'divorce settlement' had been agreed, on citizens' rights, on the divorce bill, and on the status of the Irish border, and progress on agreeing these was painfully slow. The British Government published several position papers in the summer of 2017, but many details were left vague. May attempted to break the logjam in the talks in a speech in Florence in September 2017, but her offer on the UK's budget contribution was deemed insufficient by EU Leaders. Many observers at that time believed that a deal would eventually be done both on the divorce settlement and on a trade deal, but that it would be largely on EU terms, and the trade deal would not be finalised before Britain's exit, and that the likely transition period would be too short (Grant 2017). Agreement on the divorce settlement and the transition period were agreed at meetings of the European Council in December 2017 and March 2018, but only after Britain made major concessions and discussion of the most difficult issues was postponed.

Some longer-term implications of Brexit

One of the motivations of those who led the Leave campaign was to halt the creeping Europeanisation of British politics and government, to take back control, restore British sovereignty and the accountability of Parliament to the British people, and in this way to make Britain great again. From this perspective Brexit is about restoring and enhancing the distinctive and exceptional aspects of the UK state. How likely is this?

The picture is a mixed one. Will Brexit for example give a new lease of life to the UK multinational state? In the Referendum Scotland and Northern Ireland voted Remain, while England and Wales voted Leave. In Scotland UKIP performed poorly and all four main parties campaigned strongly for Remain. The SNP sought to use the result to argue that Scotland should not be taken out of the European Union against its will, and if the Westminster Government attempted to do so without consulting Scotland then the SNP would seek a second independence referendum. This argument may in the future have some force particularly if the negotiations fail and Britain crashed out of the EU without a deal. In the short-term the SNP made little headway, and in the 2017 general election although they remained comfortably the largest party they lost votes and seats to a resurgent Conservative party under Ruth Davidson and also to Labour. But although the immediate prospect of a second independence referendum has receded, at some stage it may return, particularly if the Brexit which now unfolds comes to be seen as damaging to Scotland. Scotland is now an increasingly separate polity and votes in significantly different ways to England. Holding Scotland within the Union remains a huge challenge for Westminster politicians and Brexit makes it that much harder.

The situation in Northern Ireland is even more complicated, because although the Democratic Unionists backed Leave and Sinn Fein backed Remain, a significant part of the Unionist vote also backed Remain giving

Remain a narrow majority. One of the reasons for the vote was the status of the border with the Republic, and the risk that a hard Brexit would entail the reimposition of a hard border between North and South, threatening the peace process and economic prosperity. Resolving this issue was made one of the three core issues in the initial Brexit negotiations. It proved the most intractable. Finding a compromise to satisfy all sides was complex as many of those with long experience of Northern Ireland politics warned. The Republic of Ireland publicly stated that it would not help to engineer a new border between North and South and proposed instead the Irish sea as the border between Ireland and the UK, allowing Northern Ireland to stay within the single market and the customs union. The May government's dependence on the Democratic Unionists ruled that out, and it was also opposed by many Conservative backbenchers. The vote for Remain in the Referendum was another sign that opinion in Northern Ireland is slowly shifting away from the connection with Britain, giving greater priority to links with the Republic. Brexit has interrupted that process and led to a new polarisation along sectarian lines. It is another example of how, far from uniting the United Kingdom around a new common purpose, Brexit has made the Union more fragile.

A second area of longer-term impact is on the constitution and on governance. Britain has long been a very centralised top-down state. Its participation in EU institutions was gradually shifting the UK policy style and governance norms. Will Brexit mean that the UK reverts to a much more distinctive and idiosyncratic set of arrangements? In the short run nothing very much will change. To simplify the process of withdrawal the Government's EU Withdrawal Bill proposed to incorporate all existing EU legislation into British law. Parliament will then consider whether or not to change any particular law. That means that very little might change, particularly if future British Governments are keen to stay as close to the EU as possible. One of the arguments for leaving the EU was to restore parliamentary sovereignty, which should mean Parliament deciding whether or not to take note of the referendum result which constitutionally was only advisory. The suggestion however that Parliament might call another referendum or reverse the referendum decision following some future general election infuriated many Leavers. 'Crush the saboteurs' was the Daily Mail's headline after May had announced the election in April 2017 (Daily Mail 2017). This kind of dilemma is present in many other fields, for example over whether to withdraw the UK from the jurisdiction of the European Court and the European Court of Human Rights. In the last twenty years Britain abandoned much of its old customary constitution (Johnson 2004). It will be hard to revive but also hard to know what the constitutional and governance implications of a post Brexit UK will be. The UK has become used to having many policy issues dealt with at the European level, where the policy style and interest group politics are very different from that at Westminster (Richardson 2017). To avoid domestic policy fiascos British governments may need to change the policy process at Westminster. But there are no signs they are thinking of doing so.

The future of referendums is also unclear. The British political class up to now has treated referendums casually, giving little attention to the circumstances under which referendums should be held, the issues for which they might be appropriate, or the thresholds which might be necessary for fundamental questions to ensure that the result of a referendum represents the settled will of the people. Instead a majority of one, whatever the turnout, is currently all that is needed to determine the outcome of British referendums, which have now twice been called to try to resolve internal party conflicts. They have rarely settled anything. In the referendum in 1975 called by the Labour Government, two thirds voted Yes. But within eight years the Labour party fought a general election with a manifesto pledge to pull Britain out of the Common Market.

A third area of longer-term impact concerns the party system. The 2017 election showed that Brexit is both a symptom of longer term trends which are realigning British politics and also a magnifier of them. It has contributed greatly to the sense of fluidity and uncertainty in Britain, which feeds through to the volatility of public opinion, and the sudden surges and equally dramatic collapses in support for particular leaders and particular parties. The referendum revealed a very divided country, but one divided not so much by class but by age, education, ethnicity, region and nation, giving rise to new political identities – cosmopolitan and communitarian. The big cities, particularly London, tended to vote Remain, smaller towns and villages tended to vote Leave. The tendency for older people to vote Leave and younger people to vote Remain was particularly pronounced, as was the tendency for those with some form of higher education to vote Remain and those without to vote Leave. These patterns were then replicated in the 2017 General Election, accounting for the surge in both Conservative and Labour support at the expense of third parties, including the Liberal Democrats, the Greens and most dramatically UKIP (Curtis 2017). One impact of Brexit has been to restore a two party system. In 2017 Labour and the Conservatives won more than 80 per cent of the vote for the first time since 1979. This may not last. It is hard to imagine one or other of the two main parties will not suffer a big fall in support at some stage, and third parties may again be the beneficiary. But Brexit has certainly reshaped the social bases and the identity of the two main parties, and this is likely to endure. 77 per cent of Labour's greatly increased individual membership are drawn from the professional middle classes, and 87 per cent of Labour members voted to Remain. The Liberal Democrats collapsed in the 2015 election after their spell in coalition, and in 2017 although they regained a few seats they lost further vote share. Brexit polarised British politics between Labour and the

Conservatives, but the picture is confused because both parties are seriously divided, and are straddling quite incompatible positions in a bid to appeal to as many voters as possible. The Liberal Democrats, the Greens and UKIP who all have much greater clarity on their position on Brexit, may start to revive again as the inconsistencies of the two main parties become exposed. But for the moment Brexit has reshaped the political map and has broken not just the link between Britain and Europe, but has also undermined the consensus on austerity.

A fourth area of longer-term impact is on political economy. In the immediate aftermath of Brexit Leavers were jubilant that the sky did not fall in and that the economy continued to grow. The warnings that a vote for Brexit would create an immediate crisis of confidence among investors and plunge the economy into an immediate recession were not borne out. The appointment of Theresa May as the new Prime Minister helped steady the markets, while the Bank of England intervened with a package of measures, including a rate cut and an increase in bond issues. The main impact of Brexit was that the pound fell sharply on the foreign exchanges, but the inflationary consequences of this were delayed until 2017. Although the short-term effect was to boost exports by the end of 2017 the balance of payments deficit was widening again (Inman and Parkington 2017).

Before the referendum there were widely divergent forecasts of the effect of Brexit on the economy. Many of the models were flawed or partial in their use of evidence (Whyman and Petrescu 2017). The economic effects of Brexit were never likely to be immediate and catastrophic as the Treasury forecasts implied. The models also left out the effects of political intervention by the financial authorities. Similarly the expectation of some Brexiters that the UK could pass seamlessly and without friction into a much more prosperous and dynamic future was also improbable. Most economists and financial analysts continued to predict that there will be significant economic costs from Brexit over the medium term. RaboBank for example in October 2017 estimated that a hard Brexit would cost the UK £400bn by 2030 or 18 per cent of GDP (Rabobank 2017). Whether Brexit does lasting damage to the UK economy depends on how quickly government and citizens adapt their behaviour to the new circumstances Brexit brings. One of the ironies of the Brexit vote is that the areas likely to adjust most quickly and suffer least long-term damage are the areas which voted Remain, while the areas which voted Leave are likely to suffer disproportionately unless there is significant government intervention and a much more coordinated industrial strategy to assist them. That is because they have fewer young, entrepreneurial, highly educated cosmopolitan citizens and are more dependent on EU subsidies and protections which are unlikely to be fully replaced.

Some relocation of business and investment looks inevitable, and has already begun, as businesses assess the risks and the likely outcomes of the

Brexit negotiations. But there will be many new opportunities as well for particular sectors and companies. The economy will be reshaped by the different pressures which the Brexit process will bring about. The 20 per cent fall in the value of the £ after the Referendum result is one of the forces bringing about that change. An economy as large and as flexible as the UK's will find ways to prosper after Brexit because although there will be losers there will also be winners. But those who take this optimistic view of Brexit also tend to think that the surest way for the potential of Brexit to be realised is for it to be as hard and as clean as possible. Only if Brexit delivers a sharp shock to traditional ways of doing things is it likely to have a beneficial effect. The economic and political risks of a hard Brexit and a cliff edge mean however that most of British business lobbied hard during 2017 and 2018 to ensure that Brexit was as painless as possible by changing as little as possible in the UK's present relationship with the EU.

Business was divided over the merits of Brexit and is still more sharply divided over whether the UK should seek a hard or a soft Brexit. Most large industrial and financial companies, particularly those involved in the euro clearing markets, were opposed to Brexit, but there was a significant group of City firms, particularly hedge funds, who supported Brexit. Small businesses were more evenly divided between Leave and Remain. The trade unions mostly backed Remain, with varying degrees of enthusiasm, but all were united in opposing the globalist dream of slashing taxes, employment rights and labour market regulation in post-Brexit Britain.

The economy never operates independently of politics, although most economic models assume that it does. Assessing the impact of Brexit on the economy has to take account of political pressures, and political reactions to economic conditions. Polling evidence indicates that many Leave voters, particularly older Leave voters were prepared to accept an economic cost to achieve the Brexit they wanted (Mance 2017). The political risk run by all parties but particularly the Conservatives was that they may prove unable to deliver the kind of Brexit Leavers wanted. The risk that a no-deal would lead to an economic collapse, and the insistent lobbying of so much of British business against a hard Brexit pushes the British Government inexorably towards a soft Brexit. But that means that the actual Brexit which is delivered may be hard to distinguish from remaining full members of the European Union. The survival of the Conservative Government turns on whether it can successfully balance the competing claims of its warring party factions with the pressures from business and the EU itself. In 2018 May was seeking to keep the support of Brexiters in her party by offering a symbolic Brexit, the formal regaining of sovereignty in March 2019, while seeking at the same time to keep the support of Remainers by promising them that Britain would use its sovereignty to stay as closely aligned to the EU as possible.

A final longer-term impact of Brexit is on geopolitics and Britain's place in the world. NATO and the EU have been the bedrock of UK national security. The impact of Brexit will at best introduce uncertainty and at worst may permanently weaken western defence by introducing new divisions in Europe. There are specific issues about how a post-Brexit UK will continue to cooperate with bodies such as Europol and Euratom. It is assumed that Britain's continued participation in European security arrangements will continue after Brexit, but this is not certain. It depends on the negotiations being a success, and if the talks were to break down, many other forms of co-operation might be in peril. The election of Donald Trump further complicated matters, because Trump's evident dislike of the EU and of NATO and his support for reviving the special relationship between the UK and the US offers the UK the tempting prospect of making its relationship with the US once again the anchor for its foreign policy and its role in the post-Brexit world.

Churchill defined post-war Britain as being at the centre of three circles – Empire, Anglo-America and Europe. For post Brexit Britain there is no way to revive Empire and it is leaving Europe. Anglo-America and the wider Anglosphere offer Britain's best hope to redefine itself after Brexit and find external support to safeguard its domestic political union (Kenny and Pearce 2018) But relying on the Trump presidency is likely to bring disappointment. The nativist and isolationist strand in Trump's thinking (Laderman and Simms 2017) makes him an unreliable partner for a British Government which is globalist and wants to reaffirm its support for free trade and the international market order. Brexit is therefore likely to entail a diminution in Britain's influence and diplomatic weight in the world. The UK remains a member of the G7 and the G20 and has one of the five permanent seats on the UN Security Council. But it will no longer be part of the decision-making process of the EU and its relationship with the US is highly unequal.

Conclusion

Brexit has already had a substantial political impact on the UK, ending and advancing political careers, realigning the political parties, injecting a new populism into British politics, further destabilising the Union, and arousing fears that Britain may become less open, less diverse, and less liberal. There is dispute over whether Brexit will continue to be a disruptive force or whether its importance will now gradually subside. Much depends on what kind of Brexit finally emerges from the negotiations, and who will be most disappointed by the outcome. The costs of not delivering a Brexit which is endorsed by those Leavers for whom Brexit is the preeminent political issue could undermine democratic legitimacy and lead to restoration of the fortunes of UKIP or some successor party. But it is hard to see how this can be avoided, since the alternative is a hard Brexit which could produce the kind of economic shock which the Treasury warned about during the referendum.

The Referendum vote and the triggering of Article 50 makes cancellation of Brexit almost impossible to accomplish politically. Only the Liberal Democrats are campaigning for that. The bid to secure some kind of associate status with the EU, inside or outside the European Economic Area, staying in some kind of customs union, is more plausible, although there is no guarantee the EU will agree. Such an outcome would mean that sovereignty would notionally have been regained, and Britain would no longer participate in the Council of Ministers, the European Commission or the European Parliament. British passports would be blue again, although without the hard covers and large format of the pre-Common Market passports. Britain would have negotiated access to the single market and agreed a regular payment into the EU budget. Britain would have sovereign control over its borders, but it would exercise that sovereignty to admit as many workers from Europe as it does currently, reflecting the needs of the economy. Many Conservative MPs who supported Leave will be content if the European Court no longer has jurisdiction over the UK. Formal legal sovereignty may return but real political sovereignty will not. The impact of Brexit will be to reduce still further Britain's influence and ability to shape the rules which govern its trade. After Brexit it will become even more a rule taker rather than a rule maker.

Britain's relationship with the EU will still be a major concern of British politics after Brexit. There will still be a tendency to blame the EU for anything bad that happens to Britain. Brexiters claim that Britain is leaving the EU not leaving Europe, but that remains to be seen. Many relationships will be more difficult and permanent damage may have been done to how Britain is perceived by European citizens and still more by European politicians. The long-term impact on British domestic policy is intriguing and paradoxical. Many of the leaders of the Leave campaign wagered that exiting the EU would deliver Thatcherism MkII. But the conditions are not propitious, and what Leavers overlook is that membership of the EU helped lock the UK into a particular form of economic liberalism. That is why Margaret Thatcher was such a strong advocate and supporter of the single market. It was one of the reasons for joining in the first place, and why so many in the Labour movement were opposed. But the populist temper which the Brexit vote has uncorked has breathed new life into anti-liberal and anti-capitalist forces in Britain, and shattered the Thatcherite and the Blairite consensus, and may force a radical rethinking of the UK's economic model (Munchau 2017). It might even mean that the UK becomes more European rather than less in the future. This may be one of the more lasting and paradoxical impacts of Brexit on British politics.

Disclosure statement

No potential conflict of interest was reported by the authors.

References

Bulmer, S. and Quaglia, L. (2018) 'Introduction', Journal of European Public Policy, doi:10.1080/13501763.2018.1467957

Curtis, C. (2017) 'How Britain voted at the 2017 general election', available at https://yougov.co.uk/news/2017/06/13/how-britain-voted-2017-general-election/

Daily Mail (2017) available at http://theconversation.com/daily-mail-comes-out-fighting-as-uk-press-draws-battle-lines-for-brexit-election-76412

Dennison, J. and Geddes, A. (2018) 'Brexit and the Perils of 'Europeanised' Immigration', Journal of European Public Policy, doi:10.1080/13501763.2018.1467953

Fox, L. (2016) available at http://www.telegraph.co.uk/business/2016/09/09/british-business-fat-and-lazy-liam-fox-claims/

Grant, C. (2017) 'How Brexit will unfold: Britain will get a deal but it will come at a price', available at http://www.cer.eu/in-the-press/how-brexit-will-unfold-%E2%80%93-britain-will-get-deal-itll-come-price

Hanretty, C. (2016) available at https://medium.com/@chrishanretty/revised-estimates-of-leave-vote-share-in-westminster-constituencies-c4612f06319d

Hattersley, R. (2017) 'The Reformation should have been a warning to Remainers', available at https://www.theguardian.com/books/2017/mar/03/point-of-view-brexit-roy-hattersley-reformation

Inman, P. and Parkington, R. (2017) 'British exports outside EU fall despite weak pound', available at https://www.theguardian.com/business/2017/sep/08/uk-exports-eu-weak-pound-trade-Europe

Johnson, N. (2004) Reshaping the British Constitution: Essays in Political Interpretation, London: Palgrave-Macmillan.

Kenny, M. and Pearce, N. (2018) Shadows of Empire, Cambridge: Polity.

Laderman, C. and Simms, B. (2017) Donald Trump: The Making of a World View, London: Endeavour.

Mance, Henry (2017) 'Most Brexiters say economic damage is a price worth paying', available at https://www.ft.com/content/1b636ba8-76b3-11e7-a3e8-60495fe6ca71

Munchau, W. (2017) After Brexit, the UK's old fashioned economy will lose its clout, available at https://www.ft.com/content/fe5edeb0-cbb3-11e7-aa33-c63fdc9b8c6c

Patient, R. (2017) 'The business elite need to get their heads around the Second Glorious Revolution' http://brexitcentral.com/business-elite-second-glorious-revolution/

Qvortrup, M. (2005) A Comparative Study of Referendums: Government by the People, Manchester: Manchester University Press.

Rabobank. (2017) 'Hard Brexit to cost UK economy £400bn by 2030' https://www.rabobank.com/en/press/search/2017/20171012-brexit-scenariostudie.html

Richardson, J. (2017) 'Brexit policy-making: the need for a change in policy style', available at http://www.europeanfutures.ed.ac.uk/article-4889

Shipman, T. (2016) *All Out War: The Full Story of How Brexit Sank Britain's British Political Class*, London: William Collins.

Tusk, D. (2017) available at https://www.theguardian.com/politics/2016/oct/13/its-hard-brexit-or-no-brexit-at-all-says-eu-council-president

Whyman, P. and Petrescu, A. (2017) *The Economics of Brexit: A Cost Benefit Analysis of the UK's Economic Relationship with the EU*, London: Palgrave-Macmillan.

Index

For Product Safety Concerns and Information please contact our EU
representative GPSR@taylorandfrancis.com
Taylor & Francis Verlag GmbH, Kaufingerstraße 24, 80331 München, Germany